SINGLED OUT

Practical Wisdom and Guidance for Single Parents Navigating
Life and Entrepreneurship

Written By
Veronica White

AMARO GROUP
——— P U B L I S H I N G

Mt Pleasant, SC

www.AmaroGroupServices.com

SINGLED OUT

Paperback ISBN: 978-1-961673-07-6

Table of Contents

Forward

In a perfect world where parenthood is often portrayed as a shared journey, the reality of being a single parent can sometimes go unseen. In "Singled Out" you are about to embark on a heartfelt journey through the life and acts of a remarkable, outstanding woman who happens to be my sister. Through her courageous tales and challenges coming from the Southside of Chicago being a single parent, losing a child and her unique journey of being an entrepreneur, philanthropist and finishing school with a master's degree you will witness the resilience, strength, and unwavering love that defines her story.

Prepare to be inspired by her steadfast determination, touched by her moments of vulnerability and uplifted by her unfaltering spirit in the face of adversity. As you delve into the pages of "Singled Out," you may find solace, wisdom, and perhaps a reflection of your own journey within the pages of this powerful narrative. May this book serve as a beacon of hope for all those who have faced adversity. May these few pages give you comfort, inspiration and solidarity for all those who walk the path of single parenthood and be a reminder that even in the toughest of times love, courage and faith can light the way forward.

Calvin Daniels

Introduction

"You may not control all the events that happen to you, but you can decide not to be reduced by them."
— Maya Angelou

I am a testament to resilience, my life woven with challenges, triumphs, and a relentless commitment to personal growth. Born at Chicago's Cook County Hospital, my journey began with an inherent determination to rise above adversity and make a meaningful imprint on the world. My early years were marked by my parents' separation and my education at St. Raphael Catholic School. These experiences, along with treasured moments spent with my father and siblings, shaped the woman I am today. Life took unexpected turns when my dad had some challenges that led to incarceration; this affected me in many ways, including disruptions in education and personal development. Despite the hardships encountered during those years, I persevered and graduated from Hyde Park South high school with honors and furthered my education at Kennedy King College. Throughout my educational journey, I honed leadership skills and discovered a passion for personal finance.

Becoming a parent marked a significant chapter in my life, and I balanced raising children with pursuing education and employment, highlighting resilience and commitment. Tragedy struck with the loss of one of my daughters, a painful experience that drove me to support my community through various initiatives.

I have also embarked on entrepreneurial ventures, including starting trucking and factoring companies, and embraced opportunities to make a positive impact. My journey of growth and giving back continued, leading to milestones such as earning a master's degree in accounting and investing in real estate. Balancing business pursuits with philanthropy, I have donated thousands of school supplies, created podcasts, and learned valuable life skills, including forgiveness, personal finance, and investment.

Reflecting on my life's journey, I take pride in my transformation into a strong, compassionate, and determined individual. I am looking forward to exploring new opportunities, inspiring others, and continuing to make a positive impact on the world. As said earlier, my journey was not without challenges, including becoming a single mother at an early age and the tragic loss of my daughter. I have highlighted the importance of community support in my transformation, and I desire to become a resource for others. I aim to share stories, tools, and techniques to help others on their self-journey and build a community of people helping each other.

Setting the stage for the importance of challenges in personal growth and development

Picture this: A vast landscape stretching before you, filled with opportunities and challenges waiting to be conquered. Life is like a thrilling adventure, full of twists and turns that evaluate our strength and resilience. Challenges are not roadblocks but steppingstones towards personal growth and development. They push us out of our comfort zones, encouraging us to tap into our hidden potential and discover what we are truly capable of.

As we navigate through life, challenges become our teachers, guiding us toward self-discovery and inner strength. Embracing these challenges is a powerful way to unlock new possibilities and transform ourselves in ways we never thought possible. Each obstacle we face is an opportunity to gain experience, grow, and evolve into the best version of ourselves.

Sometimes, the path may seem uncertain, and the obstacles overwhelming. But it is in these moments of doubt and fear that we find the courage to push forward and overcome whatever stands in our way. Challenges are not meant to break us but to build us up, to shape us into resilient individuals capable of weathering any storm.

So, as we embark on this journey of self-discovery and personal growth, let us embrace challenges with open arms and a determined spirit. Let us welcome the opportunity to stretch beyond our limits and forge our path toward a brighter, more fulfilling future. Together, let us rise to the challenge and discover the true extent of our potential.

Childhood Reflections

Growing up, my childhood was filled with moments that unknowingly laid the foundation for how I would approach challenges later in life. These early experiences shaped my attitude toward challenges. Some challenges filled me with excitement and determination, while others brought fear and uncertainty. I also learned that how I responded to challenges often depended on the support and encouragement I received from those around me.

As a child, I was still figuring out how to navigate the world and make sense of my place in it. Challenges were like puzzles waiting to be solved, and each success or setback taught me something new about myself and the world around me. While some challenges left me feeling defeated and discouraged, others ignited a spark of curiosity and resilience within me.

Reflecting on my childhood now, I realize those early experiences planted the seeds of growth and development that continue to shape my approach to challenges today. Each challenge, no matter how big or small, became an opportunity for me to learn, grow, and become the person I am today.

Exploring early experiences and how they shaped attitudes towards challenges

As a child, many challenges evaluated my resilience and determination in their way. It could be learning how to ride a bike without training wheels or mustering the courage to speak up in class, each hurdle presented an opportunity for growth. These things were challenges to me as a young child and they taught me the importance of perseverance and the value of pushing past my comfort zone. Overcoming these childhood obstacles led to me developing a sense of confidence in my ability to tackle whatever life threw my way. They planted the seeds for a mindset that welcomed challenges as opportunities for personal growth.

Chapter 1

Facing Fear and Uncertainty

Life is full of moments of fear and uncertainty. These feelings can be overwhelming, causing us to question our abilities and decisions. The challenges that come our way may seem unconquerable at first, however, it is natural to feel apprehensive in situations like this. It is in these moments of vulnerability that we have the opportunity to dig deep and find the courage within ourselves to face our fears head-on. Our early experiences and how they shaped our attitudes toward challenges can provide valuable insights into how we respond to adversity. By acknowledging our initial reactions to challenges and the obstacles they present, we can better understand our triggers and patterns of behavior. It is important to recognize that it is okay to feel afraid or uncertain, as these emotions are a natural part of the human experience. However, it is crucial not to let them paralyze us or hold us back from moving forward. Instead, we can choose to confront our fears with a sense of curiosity and openness, embracing the unknown with a spirit of resilience. By acknowledging our fears and uncertainties, we can begin to dismantle their power over us, shifting our focus towards finding solutions and strategies to overcome them. This shift in perspective allows us to approach challenges with a sense of empowerment and optimism, knowing that we are capable of navigating even the most overwhelming obstacles.

Looking Ahead

As you reflect on the journey of embracing challenges and recognizing the personal growth and achievements that have resulted from them, it's natural to feel a sense of empowerment and resilience within you. If you look ahead, you will find there is a wealth of opportunities awaiting you, each presenting its own set of challenges to overcome. Remember, challenges are not obstacles but steppingstones towards your growth and success. With a positive mindset and a willingness to continue learning and evolving, you can face these future challenges with confidence and determination. Embrace the unknown with open arms, knowing that each challenge you conquer brings you one step closer to your ultimate goals. Keep building on the foundation of strength and resilience you have developed thus far, and you will find yourself well-equipped to navigate whatever lies ahead. Trust in your ability to adapt, learn, and grow from every experience, no matter how overwhelming it may seem. The road ahead may be filled with twists and turns, but with the lessons you have learned and the support of those around you, you are more than capable of facing whatever challenges come your way. Keep moving forward with courage and conviction, knowing that each challenge is simply an opportunity for you to shine and continue on your path toward personal growth and fulfillment.

Ultimately, facing future challenges with a positive mindset is a choice we make. By approaching obstacles with optimism, determination, and a willingness to learn, we can continue to grow and evolve on our journey toward personal fulfillment and success.

So, as we embark on this journey of self-discovery and personal growth, let us embrace challenges with open arms and a determined spirit. Let us welcome the opportunity to stretch beyond our limits and forge our path toward a brighter, more fulfilling future. Together, let us rise to the challenge and discover the true extent of our potential.

Exploring early experiences and how they shaped attitudes towards challenges

The unknown presented itself as a formidable opponent, stirring feelings of anxiety and apprehension within me. Thoughts of failure crept in, whispering doubts and insecurities. But deep down, a spark of determination flickered, urging me to face these challenges head-on.

With each obstacle that presented itself, I felt a mix of emotions fear, frustration, and a glimmer of hope. The road ahead seemed overwhelming, but something within me refused to back down. The fear of the unknown began to transform into a sense of curiosity and determination.

Navigating through the maze of uncertainties, I realized that seeking support was not a sign of weakness, but rather a display of strength. Opening up to others about my struggles allowed me to gain valuable insights and perspectives. Together, we faced the challenges head-on, united in our determination to overcome whatever obstacles came our way.

As I embraced the support of others, a sense of empowerment washed over me. No longer did I feel alone in my journey; I had a team of allies by my side, ready to offer guidance and encouragement. With their support, I found the courage to confront my fears and push through the obstacles that once seemed insurmountable.

Learning to Adapt

The unexpected challenges in my life made me realize the importance of being adaptable. It was during these times that I truly learned to adapt and navigate through the unknown. One particular experience stands out in my memory. I had encountered a major setback in my career that left me feeling lost and unsure of my next steps. It was an overwhelming moment, but I knew I had to find a way to adapt and overcome this obstacle. Seeking guidance from a mentor, I learned valuable lessons about resilience and the power of perseverance. Their wisdom and support helped me see the situation from a new perspective, allowing me to adapt and grow stronger in the process.

Through this experience, I discovered that adaptability is not just about surviving challenges, but also about thriving in the face of adversity. It is about embracing change and finding new ways to overcome obstacles. I learned that adaptability is a skill that can be developed with practice and determination. By being open to new ideas and approaches, I transformed challenges into opportunities for growth. This mindset shift enabled me to face future challenges with confidence and a sense of empowerment. Learning to adapt has been a valuable lesson that has carried me through many difficult moments, reminding me of the resilience and strength that lie within each of us.

Sharing stories of adapting to unexpected challenges and the lessons gained from them

I remember the time when I had a challenge that completely threw me off balance. It was a situation that I had never anticipated, let alone prepared for. But instead of shrinking away from it, I decided to adapt and find a way to navigate through it.

Initially, I felt overwhelmed and unsure of how to proceed. The uncertainty of the situation weighed heavily on me, casting a shadow of doubt over my capabilities. However, with each passing day, I started to see this challenge as an opportunity for growth rather than a roadblock.

I began to approach the situation with a fresh perspective, looking for creative solutions and seeking advice from those who had faced similar challenges before. I realized that adapting to unexpected challenges required flexibility and an open mind. I had to be willing to step outside of my comfort zone and explore new possibilities.

As I embraced this mindset shift, I started to experience small victories along the way. Each obstacle that I overcame served as a lesson in resilience and perseverance. I learned that adaptability is not just about reacting to challenges but also about proactively seeking ways to turn them into opportunities for personal development.

Discussing setbacks and how they paved the way for future successes

There have been times in my life when setbacks seemed overwhelming. I remember a particular moment when everything I had worked so hard for came crashing down around me. It felt like the end of the road like all my efforts had been for nothing. But as I look back on that difficult time now, I realize that it was a turning point in my journey.

In my setbacks, I found a strength within me that I never knew existed. I discovered a resilience that I hadn't tapped into before. Each setback forced me to reevaluate my goals and priorities and to make tough decisions about the direction of my life. It was a painful process, but it was also incredibly liberating.

Instead of letting my setbacks define me, I used them as steppingstones to something greater. I learned valuable lessons about perseverance, adaptability, and the importance of staying true to myself. Each setback taught me something new about who I am and what I am capable of achieving. And in the end, they paved the way for future successes that I never could have imagined.

So, if you're facing a setback right now, remember that it is not the end of the road. It is simply a detour on your journey towards something greater. Embrace the challenges, learn from them, and use them to propel yourself forward. You never know what amazing opportunities lie ahead once you overcome those setbacks.

Embracing Change

Change is inevitable. It's a constant force in our lives, shaping and reshaping our paths in ways we never imagined. Embracing change is not always easy, it can be scary, uncertain, and uncomfortable. But when we learn to see change as an opportunity for growth, a chance to evolve and become better versions of ourselves, that's when true transformation occurs.

Think about a time in your life when everything was falling apart. You faced a major setback, a loss, or a difficult challenge that evaluated your resilience. In those moments of darkness, it's easy to feel overwhelmed and defeated. But what if, instead of resisting change, you embraced it? What if you saw that setback as a steppingstone to something greater, a turning point that could lead to new opportunities and possibilities?

Embracing change requires a shift in mindset. It's about reframing how we view challenges, seeing them not as obstacles to overcome but as paths to growth and self-discovery. When we embrace change, we open ourselves up to new experiences, perspectives, and possibilities. We let go of fear and resistance, welcoming whatever life throws our way with an open heart and a willingness to learn and grow.

Change can be scary, yes. It can push us out of our comfort zones and into the unknown. But it is also where magic happens, where we discover our true strength and resilience. By embracing change, we permit ourselves to transform, to evolve, and to become the best version of ourselves. So, the next time change comes knocking at your door, embrace it with open arms and trust that it will lead you to new horizons you never thought possible.

Exploring the mindset shift towards seeing challenges as opportunities for growth

When faced with challenges, it's easy to feel overwhelmed and defeated. It's natural to want to avoid difficult situations or obstacles that come our way. But what if we shift our perspective and see challenges as opportunities for growth? What if we view them as chances to learn, evolve, and become stronger?

Embracing change in this way requires a shift in mindset. Instead of seeing challenges as roadblocks, we can see them as steppingstones on the path to success. Each challenge we face presents us with an opportunity to evaluate our limits, push ourselves beyond what we thought possible, and discover new strengths within us.

Cultivating resilience plays a crucial role in this process. Resilience is the ability to bounce back from setbacks, adapt to change, and persevere in the face of adversity. By developing our resilience, we can navigate challenges with grace and determination, knowing that we have the inner strength to overcome whatever comes our way.

As we embrace the mindset shift towards seeing challenges as opportunities for growth, we open ourselves up to a world of possibilities. We become more adaptable, more confident in our abilities, and more willing to take risks in pursuit of our goals. Challenges cease to be obstacles and instead become catalysts for personal development and transformation.

So let us embrace change with open arms, viewing challenges not as threats, but as invitations to become the best versions of ourselves. Let us cultivate resilience in the face of adversity, knowing that we have the power to rise above any challenge that comes our way. And let us continue on this journey of growth and discovery, embracing challenges as the keys to unlocking our full potential.

Cultivating Resilience

As we navigate through life, we encounter various challenges that evaluate our strength and resilience. Cultivating resilience is an essential skill that allows us to bounce back from difficult situations with grace and determination. It is about developing the mental toughness to face adversity head-on and emerge stronger on the other side.

One key aspect of building resilience is maintaining a positive outlook, even in the face of challenges. By reframing difficulties as opportunities for growth and learning, we can shift our perspective and approach challenges with a sense of hope and possibility. This mindset empowers us to tackle obstacles with confidence and resilience.

Another important factor in cultivating resilience is practicing self-care and self-compassion. Taking time to nurture our physical, emotional, and mental wellbeing helps us recharge and build the inner strength needed to overcome challenges. By showing ourselves kindness and understanding, we create a supportive foundation that sustains us during tough times.

Additionally, developing a strong support system is crucial in building resilience. Surrounding yourself with caring and encouraging individuals who uplift and motivate you can make a significant difference in how you navigate challenges. Lean on your friends, family, or mentors for guidance and reassurance during tough times, knowing that you are not alone in facing adversity.

Moreover, resilience is not about avoiding difficulties but about facing them head-on and learning from them. Each challenge we encounter provides an opportunity for growth and personal development. By embracing challenges as pathways to resilience, we can strengthen our ability to overcome obstacles and thrive in the face of adversity.

Remember, resilience is not about being invincible or unaffected by challenges. It is about acknowledging our struggles, learning from them, and emerging stronger and more resilient as a result. By cultivating resilience through positivity, self-care, and a supportive network, we empower ourselves to face life's challenges with courage and resilience.

Strategies for developing resilience and bouncing back from difficult situations

When faced with difficult situations, it's important to cultivate resilience to bounce back stronger than before. One strategy for developing resilience is to practice self-care. Taking care of your physical, emotional, and mental wellbeing can provide you with the strength needed to face challenges head-on. Another important strategy is to maintain a positive mindset. By focusing on the silver linings in tough situations and learning from adversity, you can build a resilient attitude that helps you navigate through challenges. Additionally, surrounding yourself with a supportive network of friends, family, or mentors can provide you with the encouragement and guidance needed to overcome obstacles. Remember, resilience is like a muscle – the more you work on it, the stronger it becomes.

Celebrating Progress

It's important to take a moment to celebrate each progress we've made so far in our lives. Each challenge we faced was an opportunity for growth, a chance to push ourselves beyond our perceived limits and emerge stronger on the other side.

Think back to those moments when you thought you couldn't go on when the weight of the world felt heavy on your shoulders. And yet, here you are, still standing, still moving forward. That resilience you developed, that inner strength you discovered within yourself—it's worth celebrating.

Remember the times when setbacks threatened to derail your progress? But you didn't give up. You kept pushing, kept fighting, and eventually overcame those challenges. That determination and perseverance deserve recognition.

And let's not forget the moments of triumph—the victories, big and small, that came as a result of embracing challenges head-on. Whether it was accomplishing a long-held goal, overcoming a deep fear, or simply realizing your potential, each achievement is a testament to your resilience and growth.

So, as we look back on the journey filled with ups and downs, let's take a moment to savor the progress we've made. Let's acknowledge how far we've come, how much we've learned, and how much stronger we've become through facing challenges with courage and resilience. Celebrate your progress, for you are the author of your own story, and each chapter is a testament to your strength and growth.

Recognizing personal growth and achievements resulting from embracing challenges

It's truly remarkable to see the growth and achievements that have come from embracing challenges. Each obstacle faced was an opportunity for personal development and learning, shaping us into who we are today. Remember those moments when it felt like the weight of the world was on our shoulders? Those were the moments that tested our strength and resilience, and in overcoming them, we emerged stronger and more resilient than ever before.

Take a moment to acknowledge and celebrate your progress. Think back to the challenges that you have overcome, the deadlines met, the fears conquered, and the new skills acquired. Let's celebrate the small wins along with the major victories because each one contributes to our personal growth and wellbeing.

Sharing insights on facing future challenges with a positive mindset and continued growth

When facing future challenges, it's crucial to maintain a positive mindset. The way we perceive challenges can impact how we approach them and the outcomes we achieve. Instead of viewing challenges as obstacles, we can see them as opportunities for personal growth and development.

One key aspect of maintaining a positive mindset is practicing gratitude. By focusing on the things, we are thankful for, even in the face of challenges, we shift our perspective and cultivate a sense of optimism. This can help us navigate difficult situations with resilience and grace.

It's also important to remember that challenges are a natural part of life. Instead of fearing them, we can embrace them as opportunities to learn, adapt, and evolve. Each challenge we overcome builds our confidence and prepares us for future obstacles.

As we continue to grow and face new challenges, it's essential to stay connected to our support network. Surrounding ourselves with positive and encouraging people can provide the strength and encouragement needed to persevere in the face of adversity.

Ultimately, facing future challenges with a positive mindset is a choice we make. By approaching obstacles with optimism, determination, and a willingness to learn, we can continue to grow and evolve on our journey toward personal fulfillment and success.

Discussing initial reactions to challenges and the obstacles they presented

In the face of fear and uncertainty, my initial reaction was one of hesitance and doubt. I questioned myself.

Thoughts of failure crept in, whispering doubts and insecurities. However, deep down, a spark of determination flickered, urging me to face these challenges.

With each obstacle that presented itself, I felt a mix of emotions. The road ahead seemed overwhelming, but something within me refused to back down. The fear of the unknown began to transform into a sense of curiosity and determination.

Seeking Support

Amidst these overwhelming challenges, it became clear that I needed to seek support. It was a humbling realization, but I knew that I couldn't navigate this difficult terrain alone. I reached out to friends, family, and mentors, sharing my struggles and seeking their guidance. Their words of encouragement and understanding provided a much-needed lifeline during those dark times.

I learned that asking for help was not a sign of weakness, but a courageous act of self-awareness. It takes strength to admit when you need assistance, and even greater courage to accept it. The support I received was a beacon of light amid my storm, offering me comfort and perspective when I felt lost and overwhelmed.

Through the kindness and wisdom of others, I gained a renewed sense of hope and resilience. Their guidance helped me see my challenges from different angles, offering fresh insights and strategies for overcoming them. Together, we brainstormed solutions, shared stories of perseverance, and celebrated small victories along the way.

Seeking support was not just about finding answers to my problems; it was about fostering connections, and building a community of care, and understanding. It reminded me that I was not alone in my struggles and that there were people who genuinely cared about my well-being. Their presence gave me strength and motivation to keep pushing forward, knowing that I had a network of support to lean on when times get tough.

Highlighting the importance of seeking help and guidance during challenging times

When facing challenges, it's easy to feel like we have to navigate through them alone. We may believe that seeking help is a sign of weakness or that we should be able to handle everything on our own. However, the truth is that seeking support and guidance during difficult times is not a sign of weakness but rather a display of strength.

Reaching out to others for help is a powerful act of self-care. It allows us to gain new perspectives, insights, and resources that we may not have considered on our own. Whether it's talking to a trusted friend, seeking advice from a mentor, or working with a professional, opening up about our challenges can bring a sense of relief and clarity.

By seeking support, we can tap into a wealth of knowledge and experience that can help us navigate through challenging times more effectively. We don't have to have all the answers ourselves, and reaching out for help can lead to better solutions and outcomes than we could have achieved alone.

Learning to ask for help is a valuable skill that not only benefits us but also strengthens our relationships with others. It fosters a sense of trust and vulnerability that can deepen connections and create a support network that sustains us through tough times.

So, if you're facing a challenge right now, remember that it's okay to reach out for help. Let go of any feelings of pride or shame and embrace the power of seeking support. You'll be amazed at how much stronger you feel when you allow others to help carry the load.

Chapter 2

Early Struggles and Self-Discovery

My mom had me when she was seventeen years old, still in high school, and my dad was twenty years old. They split up when I was three years old, and we bounced around between my mom's family members for a stable place to live. Strangely, amidst the chaos, I found solace in Catholic school, thanks to my mom's determination. Even though my parents were apart, my dad remained a steady presence in my life.

On my fifth birthday, a careless act with fireworks left me with third-degree burns and a lifelong aversion to dresses. Then, at nine, my world was shattered when my dad went to jail, and I had to redo the fourth grade. Moving in with my dad when I was ten and a half was a fresh start but brought its challenges.

High school proved tumultuous as I was kicked out twice, once for fighting and another time due to discrepancies in addresses. I refused to follow the crowd, even when my friends ventured into risky behaviors like drugs and early relationships. Witnessing abuse in my own family solidified my resolve never to tolerate mistreatment in a relationship.

The pivotal moment came at sixteen when my mother's boyfriend attacked her, yet she chose to stay. In a bold move, I demanded she leave the property my dad had provided. Despite initial discomfort, my dad's wisdom about the long-term consequences of my actions resonated deeply.

Childhood Memories: Shaping My Identity

Just like every child, I was a dreamer. My imagination knew no bounds, and I could spend hours lost in my little world. I cherished the moments spent playing with my siblings, creating memories that I hold dear to this day. Despite the challenges we faced, the bond we shared only grew stronger. My parents instilled in me the values of kindness, compassion, and perseverance. Their unwavering support gave me the courage to face the world with confidence. Looking back, I realize how those early experiences shaped my identity, laying the foundation for the person I would become. Each memory, whether joyful or challenging, played a role in shaping my character and guiding me on the path to self-discovery.

Turbulent Teenage Years: Finding My Voice

During my teenage years, I felt like I was constantly caught in a whirlwind of emotions and uncertainties. It was a time of immense growth and self-discovery, but also a period filled with confusion and inner turmoil. I struggled to find my place in the world and understand who I truly was.

During my teenage years, I began to realize the importance of standing up for myself and speaking my truth. I started to question societal norms and challenge the status quo, recognizing that my voice mattered and deserved to be heard. It was a liberating and empowering realization that paved the way for me to embrace my uniqueness and authenticity.

Through the ups and downs of my turbulent teenage years, I began to cultivate a sense of resilience and inner strength. I learned to navigate the choppy waters of adolescence with courage and grace, gaining a deeper understanding of myself and the world around me. It was during this transformative period that I embarked on a journey towards finding my voice, a journey that would shape the person I was destined to become.

Education and Career Crossroads: Navigating Uncertainty

I remember feeling overwhelmed as I approached the end of high school. The pressure to choose a career path and pursue higher education seemed like an overwhelming task. Everyone around me seemed so sure of what they wanted to do, while I was still grappling with uncertainty.

I spent countless hours researching different fields and exploring various options. Each path I considered brought its own set of challenges and rewards. It was a period of deep self-reflection and soul-searching as I tried to understand my strengths, weaknesses, and passions.

As I navigated through the sea of possibilities, I faced moments of doubt and fear. What if I made the wrong choice? Would I be able to succeed in a competitive job market? These questions loomed over me like a dark cloud, casting shadows of doubt on my future.

Despite the uncertainty, I knew that I had to take a leap of faith and trust in my abilities. I sought guidance from mentors, friends, and family members who offered valuable insights and support. Their encouragement helped me stay focused and determined to find a path that resonated with my aspirations.

Finally, after much contemplation and introspection, I made a decision that felt right in my heart. I chose a career path that aligned with my interests and values, knowing that the road ahead would be filled with challenges and opportunities for growth.

Looking back, the journey through education and career crossroads taught me valuable lessons about resilience, perseverance, and the importance of following my intuition. It was a period of uncertainty and self-discovery that shaped the person I am today.

Relationship Challenges: Heartbreaks and Lessons Learned

Navigating the tumultuous waters of relationships was never easy for me. I often found myself caught up in whirlwinds of emotions, trying to make sense of the twists and turns that love brought into my life. Heartbreaks were not unfamiliar territory, each one leaving a scar that took a lifetime to heal.

I remember the first time my heart was shattered into a million pieces. It felt like the end of the world, like I would never be able to piece myself back together again. But as time passed and I slowly picked up the fragments of my broken heart, I realized that there was a lesson in every tear shed, in every painful goodbye.

Through each relationship challenge, I learned more about myself than I ever could have imagined. I discovered my strengths and weaknesses, my boundaries, and my desires. I learned the importance of communication, honesty, and compromise. I realized that love was not just about grand gestures and passionate moments, but about the everyday choices we make to show up for each other.

But perhaps the most valuable lesson I learned from my relationship challenges was the importance of self-love. Amid heartbreak and disappointment, I found solace in nurturing a relationship with myself. I learned to appreciate my worth and to value my happiness above all else. And in doing so, I attracted healthier, more fulfilling relationships into my life.

I am grateful for the growth these heartbreaks and lessons have brought into my life. Each relationship challenge was a steppingstone on my journey to self-discovery and self-love.

I tried to fight these battles on my own, afraid to show any vulnerability or admit that I needed help. But the more I tried to push through on my own, the harder it became to keep going. It was a vicious cycle that seemed never-ending.

Eventually, I realized that seeking understanding and support was not a sign of weakness, but rather a strength. I reached out to loved ones, therapists, support groups, or anyone who could help me navigate the turbulent waters of my mind.

Seeking understanding and support was not an admission of defeat, but a powerful act of self-love. It allowed me to unravel the complexities of my mind, to confront my fears and insecurities, and to emerge stronger on the other side.

Self-discovery Journey: Uncovering Hidden Talents and Passions

Through my journey of self-discovery, I stumbled upon hidden talents and passions that had been dormant within me for years. It wasn't until I embraced my vulnerabilities and allowed myself to break down the walls, I had built around my heart that these hidden aspects of myself began to surface.

As I delved deeper into activities that brought me joy and fulfillment, I started to uncover a love for painting that I had suppressed for so long. The act of putting brush on canvas allowed me to express emotions and thoughts that I had kept buried inside. Each stroke of color brought a sense of liberation and creativity that I had been missing in my life.

In addition to painting, I also discovered a passion for writing. Words had a way of flowing effortlessly from my mind to the page, helping me make sense of my experiences and emotions in a way that had previously eluded me. Writing became a form of therapy, a way for me to process my thoughts and feelings safely and constructively.

Through my self-discovery journey, I learned the importance of exploring different aspects of myself and embracing those that resonated most deeply with me. By allowing myself to be vulnerable and open to new experiences, I was able to uncover hidden talents and passions that brought color and meaning to my life.

Embracing Vulnerability: Breaking Down Walls

During my self-discovery journey, I realized that embracing vulnerability was key to breaking down the walls I had built around me. It was scary at first, exposing my true self to others and allowing myself to be seen without masks or pretenses. But as I began to open up and share my vulnerabilities, it created deeper connections with those around me.

I learned that vulnerability was not a sign of weakness, but rather a strength. It takes courage to show your true self, flaws, and all, and to be open to whatever comes your way. By allowing myself to be vulnerable, I started to see the walls I had put up around me slowly crumble, revealing a more authentic version of myself.

Through this process, I discovered that vulnerability is not only a way to connect with others on a deeper level but also a means of self-acceptance and growth. It allowed me to be more compassionate towards myself and others, and to embrace imperfections as part of the human experience.

As I continued to embrace vulnerability, it opened up new opportunities for personal and creative growth. I was able to tap into hidden parts of myself that I had previously ignored or suppressed, leading to new insights and discoveries about who I truly am.

Breaking down walls and embracing vulnerability was not always easy, but it was a necessary step in my journey toward self-discovery and personal fulfillment. It allowed me to let go of fear and insecurity, and instead, step into my power and strength. By embracing vulnerability, I was able to uncover a deeper sense of authenticity and purpose in my life.

Chapter 3

Forgiveness:
A Path to Healing

My journey began when I was nineteen years old with the birth of my son. At twenty-one, I had a set of twins, and before my twenty-second birthday, I faced the unimaginable tragedy of losing my youngest child. The grief was overwhelming, and it felt as though time stood still. One day, I had a heart-to-heart with myself. I realized I had been lost in mourning for too long. "I know you're hurting," I told myself, understanding the depth of my pain, "but you still have two children who need you. They don't understand what's happening. They deserve a mother who is present, who will love and support them no matter what. You need to get up. If you can't do it for yourself, then do it for them." This was the moment I decided to give my children the life their sister couldn't have and be the best parent I could.

From that day forward, I resolved not to dwell in the past but to dream and work tirelessly to provide for my children. This journey wasn't easy, but I leaned heavily on my faith. Things didn't always go as planned, but I raised two positive, productive citizens whom I love, respect, and admire.

I'm not suggesting that being a single parent is easy. Like many, I had dreams of marriage, of not having to take this journey alone. But life had other plans, and I haven't married yet. Does that mean I should stop living? No. I continue to strive and achieve, despite the odds.

As a single parent, I juggled raising two children, attending school full-time, and working full-time. I'm honestly not sure how I managed, but I was driven by my determination, and my faith gave me strength.

I want to share this message: You have the same inner strength. You can dust yourself off and live another day. You don't have to remain the person you were yesterday; you can become the person you aspire to be. It takes effort, trust in your faith, and belief in yourself.

Writing this book as a single parent who has faced significant challenges, I am living proof that hardships don't have to halt your dreams. Through my journey, I learned about managing credit, excelled academically to make the dean's list, and honed my negotiation skills to buy a car and property. I have grown to respect and love myself, to give love and respect to others, and to avoid negativity. I focus on the positives I want to attract into my life because what you focus on grows. I take responsibility for my circumstances and know that I am the only one who can change them. I strive to be better every day, to be present, and to eagerly anticipate all the wonderful opportunities that lie ahead.

Through my journey, I learned the power of resilience, the importance of faith, and the enduring strength that lies within each of us. I share my story not as a tale of triumph, but as a testament to the transformative power of forgiveness and the unwavering belief that we can rise above our circumstances, no matter how difficult they may seem.

Understanding the Weight of Resentment

Resentment is like a heavy burden that we carry with us every day, weighing us down and clouding our perspective. It starts small, a seed of discontent planted by an offense or betrayal. But over time, if left unchecked, it grows into a tangled web of emotions that can consume us.

We replay the hurtful moments in our minds, allowing the pain to fester and grow. We hold onto grudges and grievances, allowing them to shape our interactions with others. Resentment colors our thoughts, distorting our perceptions and preventing us from fully experiencing joy and connection.

The weight of resentment is not just emotional it can also manifest physically, affecting our health and wellbeing. Stress, anxiety, and anger build up inside us, creating a toxic environment that can lead to physical ailments and chronic conditions.

To truly understand the weight of resentment, we must acknowledge the toll it takes on our mental, emotional, and physical health. Only then can we begin to see the importance of finding forgiveness. It is only by releasing this heavy burden that we can truly free ourselves from its grip and move forward toward healing and inner peace.

Letting Go of Past Hurts

Forgiveness is not an easy task. It requires us to dig deep within ourselves and confront the pain and resentment that we have been holding onto for so long. It's like carrying a heavy burden on our shoulders, weighing us down and affecting every aspect of our lives. But the truth is, holding onto the past only hurts us more in the long run.

When we cling to past hurts, we give power to the people or situations that caused us pain. We allow them to control our emotions and dictate our present and future. But by letting go of past hurts, we take back that power. We free ourselves from the chains of resentment and anger, and we open ourselves up to healing and growth.

Letting go of past hurts doesn't mean forgetting or condoning the actions that caused us pain. It means acknowledging the hurt, accepting it, and choosing to release it. It is a conscious decision to no longer let the past define us or hold us back. It is a powerful act of self-love and self-preservation.

When we let go of past hurts, we create space for compassion to enter our hearts. Compassion for ourselves, for the mistakes we've made and the pain we've endured. Compassion for others, understanding that they too are flawed and imperfect. It is through this compassion that we can truly begin to heal and move forward.

So, dear reader, I urge you to take a deep breath and release the weight of resentment that you have been carrying. Allow yourself the gift of letting go of past hurts and embrace the freedom and peace that forgiveness brings. It is a journey worth taking, a journey towards a lighter heart and a brighter future.

Compassion for Yourself and Others

Compassion is a powerful tool that can help us navigate through the rough waters of life. When we practice compassion for ourselves and others, we open the door to healing and understanding. It's about extending grace and kindness to us and acknowledging that we are human and prone to mistakes. At the same time, it's about recognizing that others are on their journey, with their struggles and challenges. By showing compassion, we can cultivate a sense of empathy and connection with those around us. It allows us to let go of judgment and criticism, replacing it with love and acceptance. So, as you continue on your journey of forgiveness and healing, remember to approach yourself and others with compassion and understanding.

Healing Wounds through Forgiveness

Healing wounds through forgiveness is like mending the broken pieces of a shattered vase – it takes time, patience, and a gentle touch. As you navigate the delicate process of forgiveness, remember that it's not just about absolving others of their wrongdoings; it's also about granting yourself the gift of inner peace.

When you choose to release the grip of anger and resentment, you open up space in your heart for healing to take place. Allow yourself to acknowledge the pain and hurt that you've experienced, but also recognize that holding onto these emotions only prolongs your suffering.

Forgiveness is a powerful tool that can help you break free from the chains of the past. By choosing to let go of negative feelings towards yourself and others, you create an opportunity for growth and transformation. Remember that forgiveness is a journey, not a destination, and it's okay to take small steps toward letting go.

As you embark on the path of healing through forgiveness, be kind to yourself. Practice self-compassion and allow yourself to feel a range of emotions as you navigate this process. Trust that each step you take towards forgiveness brings you closer to a place of peace and freedom.

In the process of healing wounds through forgiveness, you may discover a newfound sense of liberation and empowerment. Embrace this transformation with an open heart and a willingness to let go of the past. By releasing negative emotions and choosing forgiveness, you pave the way for a brighter future filled with hope, love, and inner harmony.

Releasing Negative Emotions

As we continue on our journey toward healing and forgiveness, it's essential to address the negative emotions that may be weighing us down. These emotions, such as anger, resentment, and pain, can create a heavy burden on our hearts and minds. By acknowledging and releasing these negative feelings, we can pave the way for true healing and transformation.

It's normal to feel a range of emotions when we've been hurt or wronged. But holding onto these negative emotions only prolongs our suffering. By consciously choosing to let go of anger and resentment, we free ourselves from their grip and create space for healing to take place.

One way to release negative emotions is through introspection and self-awareness. Take the time to reflect on the root causes of your pain and anger. By understanding the source of these emotions, you can begin the process of releasing them.

Practicing mindfulness and meditation can also be powerful tools for letting go of negative emotions. By focusing on the present moment and tuning into your thoughts and feelings without judgment, you can create a sense of inner peace and calm.

Forgiveness is not about condoning the actions of others or forgetting the hurt they caused. It's about freeing yourself from the burden of carrying around negative emotions and releasing the power that the past holds over you.

As you work towards releasing negative emotions, remember to be patient and gentle with yourself. Healing is a journey, and it takes time to let go of deep-seated pain and anger. Trust in the process and have faith that with each step you take towards forgiveness, you are moving closer to a place of peace and freedom.

By releasing negative emotions, you are making room for positivity, love, and light to enter your life. Embrace this transformation with an open heart and a willingness to let go of the past. As you release what no longer serves you, you create space for new beginnings and a brighter future ahead.

Moving Forward with a Lighter Heart

As you release those negative emotions that have weighed you down for so long, you may start to feel a sense of light washing over you. It's like shedding a heavy coat that you've been carrying around, allowing you to move more freely and effortlessly. This newfound lightness can bring a sense of relief and liberation as if a burden has been lifted off your shoulders.

With this lightness comes a sense of clarity and peace. You may find that your mind is no longer clouded by anger, resentment, or hurt. Instead, there is room for more positive thoughts and feelings to enter. You may begin to see things from a new perspective, one that is not clouded by negative emotions but rather illuminated by understanding and compassion.

As you move forward with a lighter heart, you may notice a renewed energy and enthusiasm for life. You may feel more hopeful about the future and more open to new experiences. Your relationships with others may also improve as you can come from a place of forgiveness and understanding.

This journey towards a lighter heart is not always easy, and there may still be moments when you feel the weight of the past creeping back in. But by continuing to practice forgiveness and compassion, you can keep moving forward with a sense of lightness and grace.

Remember that true healing takes time and patience and be gentle with yourself as you navigate this process.

In the moments when you feel overwhelmed or weighed down, take a deep breath, and remind yourself of how far you have already come. Celebrate the progress you have made and the strength you have shown in choosing to release those negative emotions. With a lighter heart, you are better equipped to face whatever challenges may come your way and to continue growing and evolving into the best version of yourself.

Self-reflection and Growth

Self-reflection is a powerful tool that allows us to delve deep into our inner selves and uncover truths that may be hidden beneath the surface. It is a journey of self-discovery and growth, where we take the time to examine our thoughts, actions, and beliefs with honesty and openness. Through self-reflection, we gain a greater understanding of who we are, what drives us, and where we want to go in life.

By taking the time to reflect on our past experiences, we can identify patterns and behaviors that may no longer serve us. We can acknowledge our mistakes and learn from them, using them as steppingstones towards personal growth and transformation. Self-reflection allows us to appreciate how far we have come and gives us the clarity and insight needed to move forward with intention and purpose.

As we engage in self-reflection, we gain a deeper sense of self-awareness and develop a stronger connection to our inner being. We become more attuned to our emotions, values, and beliefs, allowing us to make decisions that align with our true selves. Through this process, we cultivate a greater sense of authenticity and integrity, living in a way that is true to who we are at our core.

Self-reflection also fosters a mindset of continuous improvement and self-development. It encourages us to set goals, learn from our experiences, and strive to become the best version of ourselves. By regularly engaging in self-reflection, we create a habit of introspection that promotes personal growth and self-discovery.

In this journey of self-reflection and growth, it is important to approach ourselves with compassion and understanding. We must be gentle with ourselves, acknowledging that we are works in progress and that growth takes time. By practicing self-compassion, we can nurture a positive relationship with ourselves and cultivate a mindset of self-acceptance and love.

Through self-reflection, we can uncover our true potential and unlock the power within us to create a life filled with purpose, meaning, and fulfillment. It is a journey of self-discovery and growth that allows us to embrace our truth, embody our values, and pursue our dreams with courage and conviction.

Embracing Peace and Inner Freedom

As you continue on your journey of self-reflection and growth, it becomes increasingly clear that embracing peace and inner freedom is a crucial step in your path to forgiveness and healing. Peace is not just the absence of conflict but a state of calmness and harmony within yourself. It allows you to release the burdens of the past and focus on the present moment.

Inner freedom is the liberation of your mind and spirit from the shackles of anger, resentment, and bitterness. It is the ability to let go of negative emotions and embrace positivity and joy. Inner freedom empowers you to choose forgiveness as a path to release yourself from the pain of the past.

Embracing peace and inner freedom requires a shift in perspective and a commitment to self-care. It involves letting go of control and surrendering to the flow of life. Through acceptance and gratitude, you can cultivate a sense of peace that transcends external circumstances.

Finding inner freedom is a process of self-discovery and inner exploration. It involves connecting with your true essence and tapping into your inner strength. By acknowledging your vulnerabilities and fears, you can confront them with courage and compassion.

As you embrace peace and inner freedom, you will notice a profound transformation within yourself. Your heart will be lighter, your mind clearer, and your spirit more at ease. Forgiveness will become a natural response, born out of a place of love, and understanding.

Remember that embracing peace and inner freedom is a continuous journey, not a destination. It requires patience, persistence, and a deep commitment to your well-being. By nurturing your inner peace and freedom, you pave the way for a life filled with love, joy, and forgiveness.

Forgiving for Your Well-Being

When you choose to forgive, you are not only releasing the burden of anger and resentment from your own heart but also taking a significant step toward your well-being. Forgiveness is a powerful tool that can free you from the chains of negativity and foster a sense of peace within yourself.

By forgiving others, you are showing compassion and kindness not just to them but also to yourself. Holding onto grudges and bitterness only poisons your soul, while forgiveness allows you to let go of that toxicity and embrace positivity instead.

Forgiveness is not about excusing the actions of others or pretending that the hurt they caused didn't matter. It is about acknowledging the pain, accepting it, and then making the conscious choice to release it. In doing so, you are reclaiming your power and refusing to let past hurts define your present and future.

Forgiving for your well-being means choosing your own mental and emotional health above all else. It is a form of self-care that allows you to move forward with a sense of freedom and inner peace. When you forgive, you are no longer tied to the past but can focus on the present moment and create a brighter future for yourself.

Remember, forgiveness is a gift you give yourself. It is a path to healing and growth, allowing you to break free from the cycle of resentment and embrace a life filled with love, understanding, and compassion. Choose forgiveness not just for others, but for your wellbeing and happiness.

Chapter 4
Overcoming Challenges

At some point in my life, I had to take responsibility and say that I could not change my past. My present is what I'm living. My future is undetermined, so I get to change myself. I get to be whoever it is I want to be and do whatever I want to do. I have an opportunity to work on that, so I take every advantage of it, try new things, dream big, set goals, reach those, and set more. If you are reading this book, I want you to know that you have those same opportunities. You can pick yourself up, and you can say, 'This is the life I desire to have; I don't know how I'm going to have it but first, I have to dream, imagine, and know that I get to live that life. I believe I have everything in the universe to help me make that happen.' Believe this and you will achieve all that you set your mind to. I also know that I'm not in competition with another living person. I just want to be better than I was yesterday. Nowadays I just want to be better than I was the day before.

My first child's father had four daughters by several women. I had his first son who he didn't meet until my child was four years old. At that point, he didn't know how to develop a relationship with him. He would see him for his birthday and Christmas, but he wouldn't see him consistently so from the time my son was four until he graduated high school, I would call his dad every three months to let him know how he was doing and also to inform him of everything he needed. Like, a haircut, clothes, socks, T-shirts, and underclothes. I get all these for him every three months from when he was age seven to fourteen. I didn't blame my children's fathers for not participating. I recall having a conversation with him when my son was in high school asking why he chose not to participate, and he informed me that he didn't know how to take me because I never called nor cussed him out about not doing things or being there for my son. Maybe he wasn't meant to be in his life and so, I told my kids if they ever feel a certain way because their dads are not active in their lives, they should let them know. I did this because adults don't know everything and sometimes, they're going through things. Adults are usually so focused on the challenges they have and never understand how they affect other people around them. I was very clear about this to them. I also didn't want to interfere with my children's relationship with their fathers.

Understanding the Power of Habits

Habits are the building blocks of our lives. They are the small, insignificant actions that we repeat day in and day out. What we often fail to realize is the immense power that these habits hold over us. They shape our thoughts, our behaviors, and our destinies.

Think about it. How many times have you found yourself mindlessly scrolling through your phone, or reaching for that bag of chips when you're feeling stressed? These actions may seem harmless at the moment, but over time, they can have a significant impact on our well-being.

Understanding the power of habits gives us the key to unlocking lasting change in our lives. When we recognize the role that habits play in shaping our reality, we can begin to take control of our behaviors. We can choose to cultivate positive habits that support our goals and dreams, rather than being slaves to negative patterns that hold us back.

By delving deep into the mechanisms behind habits, we gain insight into how they are formed and how they can be changed. We learn that habits are not set in stone; they can be broken and replaced with healthier alternatives. This knowledge empowers us to take charge of our lives and create the future we desire.

So, take a moment to reflect on your habits. Are they leading you closer to your goals, or are they keeping you stuck in a cycle of mediocrity? Remember, you have the power to shape your habits, and in turn, shape your destiny.

Identifying Negative Patterns

Recognizing negative patterns in our lives can be a challenging but crucial step toward personal growth and positive change. These patterns are like invisible threads that weave throughout our daily routines, influencing our thoughts, actions, and emotions. Whether it's procrastination, self-doubt, negative self-talk, or unhealthy relationships, these patterns can hold us back from reaching our full potential.

One way to identify these negative patterns is to pay attention to recurring themes or behaviors that leave us feeling drained, unhappy, or unfulfilled. Take a moment to reflect on your daily habits and interactions. Are there certain situations or people that consistently trigger negative emotions or behaviors in you? Are there recurring thoughts or beliefs that undermine your self-confidence or motivation?

It's also important to examine the root causes of these negative patterns. Often, our past experiences, traumas, or conditioning play a significant role in shaping our behaviors and beliefs. By exploring these underlying factors with curiosity and compassion, we can gain insight into why we engage in certain patterns and how they impact our well-being.

Once you have identified these negative patterns, it's essential to approach them with kindness and self-awareness. Rather than judging or criticizing yourself for these behaviors, see them as opportunities for growth and transformation. Remember that change is a gradual process, and it's okay to seek support from friends, family, or a therapist as you navigate this journey.

By shining a light on these negative patterns and acknowledging their presence in your life, you are taking the first step towards breaking free from their hold. Embrace this awareness as a catalyst for positive change and a deeper understanding of yourself. Ultimately, by facing these patterns head-on, you pave the way for a brighter, more empowered future filled with growth, resilience, and self-love.

Creating a Vision for Change

Visualize where you want to be. Picture a future where you have overcome your negative patterns and are living a more fulfilling life. Close your eyes and imagine the person you want to become. What does that vision look like? What goals have you achieved? How do you feel in this new reality?

Let this vision guide your journey towards change. Use it as a beacon of hope and motivation during challenging times. Visualizing the positive outcomes of your efforts can help you stay focused and determined to make lasting improvements.

Take some time to reflect on your vision for change. Write down your goals and aspirations. Be specific about what you want to achieve and how you plan to get there. Visualize your success and let that vision inspire you to take action towards creating the life you desire.

Setting Realistic Goals

Setting realistic goals is a crucial step in your journey toward positive change. When you set goals that are attainable and aligned with your vision for the future, you are more likely to stay motivated and see progress. Consider what is important to you and what changes you want to make in your life. By breaking down your larger vision into smaller, manageable goals, you can create a roadmap for success. Remember to be specific and measurable in your goal setting, so you know when you have achieved them. Don't be afraid to adjust your goals as needed along the way, allowing for flexibility and growth. Celebrate each milestone you reach, no matter how small, as each step forward brings you closer to your ultimate vision for change.

Establishing a Routine

Creating a routine is like building a sturdy foundation for a house. It provides structure, stability, and a sense of direction in our daily lives. When we have a routine in place, we are better able to manage our time, accomplish tasks efficiently, and maintain a balanced lifestyle.

Start by identifying your priorities and the activities that bring you joy and fulfillment. Allocate time in your schedule for these activities, making them non-negotiable. Consider what time of day you are most productive and energetic and plan your most important tasks during those hours.

Consistency is key when establishing a routine. Try to wake up and go to bed at the same time each day to regulate your body's internal clock. Set specific time blocks for work, exercise, leisure, and self-care, ensuring that each aspect of your life receives the attention it deserves.

Remember that routines should be flexible and adaptable. Life is unpredictable, and unexpected events may require you to make adjustments to your schedule. Embrace these changes with a positive attitude and find ways to incorporate them into your routine without feeling overwhelmed.

As you cultivate a daily routine, pay attention to how it impacts your overall well-being. Notice any improvements in your productivity, mood, and satisfaction levels. Reflect on what is working well and what areas could use refinement. Through self-reflection, you can continually optimize your routine to best serve your needs and goals.

By establishing a consistent and balanced routine, you empower yourself to navigate life's challenges with greater ease and resilience. Embrace the process of creating a structure that supports your growth and success, one day at a time.

Practicing self-reflection

Self-reflection is a powerful tool for personal growth and development. It allows us to pause, look within, and gain insights into our thoughts, feelings, and actions. By taking the time to reflect on our experiences, we can better understand ourselves, our motivations, and our behavior. Self-reflection allows us to identify areas where we may need to make changes or improvements, leading to a more fulfilling and intentional life.

To practice self-reflection, find a quiet space where you can be alone with your thoughts. Close your eyes, take a few deep breaths, and bring your awareness to the present moment. Reflect on your day or week, considering moments of joy, challenges, and lessons learned. Ask yourself why certain events made you feel a certain way and what you can learn from them. Consider your interactions with others and how you showed up in those moments.

Journaling can be a helpful tool for self-reflection. Write down your thoughts, feelings, and observations without judgment. You may discover patterns in your behavior or uncover hidden beliefs that are holding you back. Use this process to gain clarity on your goals, values, and priorities.

Self-reflection is not always easy, as it requires us to be honest with ourselves and confront aspects of our lives that may be uncomfortable. However, the insights gained from this practice can be transformative, leading to greater self-awareness, personal growth, and a deeper connection to our inner selves. Through regular self-reflection, we can cultivate a deeper understanding of ourselves and make positive changes that align with our true selves.

Cultivating Mindfulness

Practicing mindfulness is about being fully present in the moment, and aware of your thoughts and feelings without judgment. It's about paying attention to your surroundings, body, and emotions. Cultivating mindfulness can help you reduce stress, increase self-awareness, and improve your overall wellbeing.

One way to cultivate mindfulness is through meditation. Find a quiet space, sit comfortably, and focus on your breath. Notice the sensations of each inhale and exhale, allowing thoughts to come and go without getting caught up in them.

Another way to practice mindfulness is through mindful eating. Take the time to savor each bite of your meal, noticing the flavors, textures, and smells. Be present with your food and truly experience the act of nourishing your body.

Mindfulness can also be incorporated into everyday activities. Whether you're walking, washing dishes, or talking to a friend, try to bring your full attention to the task at hand. Notice the details, engage your senses, and appreciate the moment for what it is.

By cultivating mindfulness, you can learn to respond to life's challenges with grace and clarity. You can build a deeper connection with yourself and others and find peace amid chaos. Practice mindfulness regularly and watch as it transforms your perspective and enriches your life.

Finding Accountability Partners

Finding someone to help you stay accountable can make a world of difference on your journey toward building positive habits. It's like having a cheerleader in your corner, someone who encourages you to keep going even when things get tough. Accountability partners can provide support, motivation, and a sense of accountability that can help you stay on track.

When looking for an accountability partner, seek someone who shares similar goals or values with you. This person should be someone you trust and respect, as well as someone who is committed to supporting you on your journey. You can choose a friend, family member, colleague, or even a mentor who can help keep you focused and motivated.

Communicate openly and honestly with your accountability partner about your goals, challenges, and progress. Share your successes and setbacks with them and be willing to listen to their feedback and advice. Together, you can brainstorm solutions, celebrate achievements, and provide each other with the encouragement needed to stay motivated.

Establish regular check-ins with your accountability partner to review your progress and set new goals. Whether it's a weekly phone call, a monthly meeting, or daily check-ins through text or email, having these regular touchpoints can help you stay accountable and focused on your journey toward positive change.

Remember that accountability is a two-way street. Just as your partner is there to support you, be sure to offer the same level of support and encouragement in return. Celebrate each other's successes, lift each other during challenges, and keep each other accountable for the commitments you've made.

Having an accountability partner by your side can make the process of developing positive habits more manageable and enjoyable. Together, you can cheer each other on, celebrate milestones, and keep each other motivated to reach your goals.

Celebrating Progress and Success

When it comes to developing positive habits, celebrating your progress and successes along the way is crucial. It's easy to get caught up in the process and forget to acknowledge how far you've come. Remember, every small step forward is a victory worth celebrating.

Take the time to reflect on your achievements, no matter how big or small they may seem. Whether you reached a milestone in your journey or simply stayed consistent with your new habit, give yourself a pat on the back. Acknowledge the effort and dedication you've put in, and truly savor the feeling of accomplishment.

Celebrating your progress not only boosts your confidence and motivation but also reinforces the positive habits you're trying to build. When you acknowledge and celebrate your successes, you're reinforcing the behavior and signaling to yourself that you're on the right track.

Find meaningful ways to celebrate your wins. It could be treating yourself to something you enjoy, sharing your achievements with a friend or accountability partner, or simply taking a moment to bask in the feeling of accomplishment. Allow yourself to feel proud of what you've achieved and use that positive energy to fuel your continued progress.

Bear in mind that developing positive habits is not just about the end goal; it's also about the growth and transformation you experience along the way. So, celebrate each step forward, no matter how small, and let it inspire you to keep pushing forward toward your goals.

Faith Over Fear

As we navigate through the twists and turns of life, uncertainty often looms like a dark cloud overhead. The unknown can be an overwhelming prospect, leaving us feeling lost and vulnerable. In times of uncertainty, we may find ourselves grasping for solid ground, searching for something to anchor our restless souls.

It is during these moments of doubt and fear that faith becomes a guiding light, illuminating the path ahead and offering solace to our troubled hearts. Faith is not merely a belief in the unseen; it is a powerful force that allows us to move forward with courage and conviction, despite the uncertainties that lie ahead.

Embracing faith is more than just a leap of belief; it is a conscious choice to trust in something greater than ourselves and to surrender to the unknown with open hearts and open minds. It is a willingness to let go of the need for control and certainty, and instead, embrace the mysteries of life with a sense of curiosity and wonder.

In the face of uncertainty, faith acts as a beacon of hope, guiding us through the stormy seas of doubt and fear. It gives us the courage to step into the unknown, knowing that we are supported and protected by forces beyond our understanding. Faith empowers us to face our fears, transforming them into opportunities for growth and self-discovery.

As we embark on this journey of faith, let us open our hearts to the infinite possibilities that lie ahead. Let us set aside our doubts and fears and embrace the beauty of the unknown with a spirit of curiosity and wonder. Together, let us walk hand in hand with faith as our steadfast companion, guiding us through the uncertainties of life with grace and courage.

Facing Uncertainty: Embracing Faith

Life is full of uncertainties, isn't it? We never know what tomorrow will bring, what challenges we may face, or how things will unfold. It's like walking into a dark room, not knowing what's in it with you. In those moments of uncertainty, fear can easily creep in, whispering doubts and worries into our minds. But what if, instead of succumbing to fear, we choose to embrace faith?

Faith is like a guiding light in the darkness, a beacon of hope that helps us navigate through the unknown. It's about trusting in something greater than us and believing that we are not alone in this journey. When we face uncertainty with faith, we open ourselves up to endless possibilities and opportunities. We let go of the need to control every outcome and surrender to the flow of life.

Embracing faith is not about denying our fears or pretending everything is perfect. It's about acknowledging our doubts and insecurities while choosing to trust in something beyond ourselves. It's a radical act of courage, a willingness to step into the unknown with an open heart and a steadfast belief that everything will work out in the end.

So, the next time you find yourself facing uncertainty, take a deep breath and lean into your faith. Trust that you are supported, guided, and loved unconditionally. It's in these moments of greatest uncertainty that our faith has the power to shine the brightest.

Confronting Fear: Understanding the Root Cause

Fear is a powerful force that can hold us back from reaching our full potential. It often lurks in the shadows, whispering doubts and insecurities in our minds. Have you ever stopped to think about where this fear comes from? What is its root cause?

At the core of fear lies a sense of uncertainty and vulnerability. It stems from a deep-seated concern about the unknown and the potential consequences of taking risks. Our past experiences, traumas, and societal influences all contribute to the development of our fears.

By understanding the root cause of our fears, we can begin to unravel their grip on our lives. We can peel back the layers of conditioning and negative beliefs to uncover the true source of our anxieties. This self-awareness is the first step towards conquering fear and reclaiming our sense of empowerment.

Often, fear is rooted in a fear of failure or rejection. We may have been taught to equate mistakes with weakness, leading us to avoid taking chances or pursuing our dreams. By acknowledging these underlying beliefs, we can reframe our perspective and see failures as opportunities for growth and learning.

Moreover, fear can also be fueled by a lack of self-confidence and a feeling of inadequacy. Comparison to others and unrealistic expectations can exacerbate these feelings of insecurity. By practicing self-compassion and embracing our unique strengths and talents, we can diminish the power of these fears.

Ultimately, confronting fear requires courage and a willingness to face our vulnerabilities. It is a journey of self-discovery and self-acceptance, where we learn to embrace our fears as part of our growth process. By understanding the root cause of our fears, we can transform them into sources of strength and resilience.

Cultivating Belief: Strengthening Your Faith Muscle

To conquer fear, it is crucial to focus on nurturing and strengthening our belief in ourselves and the greater forces at play in our lives. Cultivating belief is akin to exercising a muscle, the more we work on it, the stronger it becomes. It is about building up our faith and trust in the universe, in our abilities, and the power of positivity.

One way to cultivate belief is through visualization. Take some time each day to envision yourself succeeding, achieving your goals, and overcoming obstacles. See yourself as a confident and capable individual who can handle whatever comes your way. This practice can help reinforce your belief in yourself and your capabilities.

Another important aspect of strengthening your faith muscle is surrounding yourself with positive influences. Seek out like-minded individuals who support and uplift you. Engage in activities that inspire and motivate you. By immersing yourself in positivity, you are creating an environment that nurtures your belief and helps you stay focused on your goals.

Additionally, practicing gratitude can be a powerful tool in cultivating belief. Take time each day to reflect on the things you are thankful for, big or small. By acknowledging and appreciating the blessings in your life, you are shifting your focus toward abundance and positivity. This attitude of gratitude can help build a strong foundation for your faith to grow.

Cultivating belief is a continuous process. It requires dedication, patience, and resilience. But with each step you take towards strengthening your faith muscle, you are empowering yourself to face challenges with courage and optimism. Trust in yourself, trust in the journey, and trust in the power of belief to lead you towards your dreams.

Overcoming Doubt: Navigating Inner Conflicts

Doubt can be a persistent companion on our journey of faith. It creeps in when we least expect it, casting shadows of uncertainty over our beliefs and aspirations. It's like a nagging voice in the back of our minds, whispering words of doubt and undermining our confidence.

Navigating these inner conflicts requires a deep dive into the root of our doubts. We must confront the source of our uncertainties, acknowledging our fears and insecurities. By shining a light on these shadows, we can begin to unravel the tangled web of doubt that holds us back.

Sometimes, our doubts stem from past experiences or traumas that have left a mark on our hearts. These wounds can fester and grow, feeding our doubts and clouding our judgment. It's crucial to address these underlying issues, seeking healing and closure where needed.

Practicing self-reflection and mindfulness can help us identify the patterns of doubt that recur in our lives. By observing our thoughts and emotions without judgment, we can gain clarity on the sources of our doubts and begin to challenge them.

Building a support system of trusted friends, mentors, or spiritual guides can provide valuable perspectives and guidance as we navigate our doubts. Opening up to others about our struggles can help us see things from different angles and gain new insights into our beliefs.

Ultimately, overcoming doubt is a gradual process that requires patience and perseverance. It's a journey of self-discovery and growth, as we learn to trust in ourselves and the higher power that guides us. By facing our doubts and working through them with courage and resilience, we can emerge stronger and more grounded in our faith.

Seeking Guidance: Finding Wisdom in Faith

When faced with uncertainty and inner conflicts, seeking guidance can provide clarity and wisdom to navigate through challenging times. Faith is not just about believing in something greater than us; it is also about finding the strength and guidance we need to move forward.

In moments of doubt, when our minds are clouded with uncertainty, turning to faith can offer a sense of grounding and perspective. It allows us to trust in a higher power or purpose, knowing that there is a plan beyond what we can see.

Finding wisdom in faith means tapping into a source of guidance that goes beyond our understanding. It may come in the form of prayer, meditation, or seeking counsel from spiritual leaders or mentors who can offer insights from a different perspective.

Faith can be a beacon of light in times of darkness, illuminating a path forward when the way seems unclear. It provides a sense of comfort and reassurance, reminding us that we are not alone in our struggles.

When we approach challenges with faith, we can draw upon a deeper reservoir of strength and resilience. It gives us the courage to take bold steps forward, knowing that we are supported and guided every step of the way.

In seeking guidance through faith, we open ourselves up to receiving divine wisdom and insights that can help us overcome obstacles and make decisions that align with our highest good. It is a journey of trust and surrender, allowing us to release control and let go of our fears.

As we continue to walk the path of faith, we discover that wisdom is not just found in answers but also in the journey of seeking. It is a continuous process of growth and self-discovery, where we learn to trust in the unknown and embrace the unfolding of our lives with grace and courage.

Courage in Action: Taking Bold Steps Forward

As the fog of fear begins to lift, a glimmer of courage starts to shine within you. It's that quiet voice nudging you to take a step, to move forward despite the uncertainty that lingers. Courage isn't about the absence of fear; it's about taking action in the face of it. It's about acknowledging your fears and doubts, but not letting them control your decisions.

Courage is not always loud and grand; sometimes, it's found in the small, everyday choices you make. It's in the decision to speak up when your voice trembles, to try again after a setback, to believe in yourself when doubt clouds your mind. It's about recognizing that growth and progress often lie just beyond your comfort zone.

Taking bold steps forward requires a willingness to be vulnerable, to risk failure, and to trust in your resilience. It means being open to new experiences, new perspectives, and new opportunities. It's about setting aside the familiar and venturing into the unknown with a spirit of curiosity and determination.

Courage is not a one-time act but a continual practice. It's about showing up, even when you're scared, and facing each challenge with unwavering resolve. It's about daring to dream big, pursue your passions, and push past the limitations you've placed on yourself. It's about embracing the journey, with all its twists and turns, knowing that each step forward brings you closer to the person you are meant to become.

So, take a deep breath, gather your strength, and step into the unknown with courage as your guide. Trust in your abilities, trust in the wisdom you've gained, and trust in the power of taking bold steps forward. And remember, each courageous act you take is a testament to the strength and resilience that lies within you.

Gratitude in Adversity: Finding Silver Linings

Amidst the storms of life, there is always a silver lining waiting to be discovered. It's during our most challenging moments that the power of gratitude shines brightest. When we shift our focus from what we lack to what we have, miracles start to unfold. Adversity becomes a teacher, guiding us toward a deeper appreciation for the blessings that surround us.

During the chaos, finding moments of gratitude can be a beacon of light. It's those small victories, the unexpected kindness of a stranger, or the beauty of nature that remind us of the goodness in the world. In times of struggle, embracing gratitude can turn our perspective from despair to hope.

Gratitude is not just about saying thank you; it's about recognizing beauty amid chaos. It's about acknowledging the strength within us that carries us through the storms. When we practice gratitude in adversity, we cultivate resilience and inner peace. We realize that even in the darkest moments, there is light waiting to be found.

Every setback becomes an opportunity for growth, every challenge a chance to learn. Gratitude in adversity is a powerful tool that helps us navigate the rough seas of life with grace and compassion. It teaches us to see the silver linings, to find joy amid sorrow, and to be grateful for every experience that shapes us into who we are meant to be.

So, as you face challenges and setbacks, remember to pause, and find the silver linings. Embrace gratitude as your companion on the journey, guiding you through the storms and illuminating the path ahead. Amid adversity, always remember to find the blessings, for they are the true treasures that sustain us through the toughest times.

Building Resilience: Harnessing Faith as a Shield

In times of trials and tribulations, our faith can be our strongest ally. It serves as a shield, protecting us from the arrows of doubt and fear that seek to penetrate our hearts. Building resilience through the harnessing of faith is not just about weathering the storm, but about emerging stronger on the other side.

When challenges arise, it is easy to become overwhelmed and lose sight of our inner strength. But it is during these moments that our faith can become a beacon of hope, guiding us through the darkness. By anchoring ourselves in our beliefs and convictions, we can tap into a wellspring of resilience that lies deep within us.

Resilience is not about avoiding difficulties or denying their existence; it is about facing them with unwavering faith. It is about recognizing that every obstacle is an opportunity for growth and transformation. Through the lens of faith, we can see setbacks as steppingstones towards our greater purpose.

As we navigate the turbulent waters of life, faith acts as a buoy, keeping us afloat amidst the crashing waves. It reminds us that we are not alone in our struggles and that there is a higher power guiding our path. With faith as our shield, we can stand firm in the face of adversity, knowing that we have the strength and courage to overcome any storm.

In the journey of building resilience, we learn to trust in the process, surrender control, and place our faith in something greater than ourselves. It is through this act of surrender that we find true freedom and empowerment. By relinquishing our fears and doubts to the power of faith, we open ourselves up to endless possibilities and potential.

So, let us embrace the challenge of building resilience through the harnessing of faith as a shield. Let us stand tall in the face of adversity, knowing that we are fortified by our unwavering belief. With faith as our constant companion, we can weather any storm and emerge stronger, wiser, and more resilient than ever before.

Embracing the Power of Faith

Throughout our journey, we have seen the remarkable strength that can be found in embracing faith. It is not merely a shield to protect us from the storms of life but a guiding light that illuminates our path even in the darkest of times. When we harness the power of faith, we discover a reservoir of resilience within us that allows us to weather any challenge with grace and courage.

As we reflect on our experiences, we realize that faith is not just a belief in something greater than ourselves; it is a fundamental force that shapes our thoughts, actions, and our destiny. It transforms our fears into opportunities for growth, our doubts into unwavering certainty, and our struggles into steppingstones toward our dreams.

Embracing the power of faith is not a passive act but an active choice we make every day. It requires courage to trust in the unseen, to surrender control, and to relinquish our need for certainty. But in doing so, we open ourselves up to a world of infinite possibilities and miracles beyond our wildest imagination.

As we close this chapter of our journey, let us carry forward the lessons we have learned about the transformative power of faith. Let us continue to nurture our belief, cultivate resilience in the face of adversity, and walk confidently towards our dreams, knowing that we are guided and protected by a force greater than ourselves.

May we always remember that in moments of doubt, fear, or uncertainty, faith is our greatest ally. It is the steady anchor that keeps us grounded amidst the turbulence of life. So, let us embrace the power of faith with open hearts and unwavering trust, knowing that with this potent force by our side, we are capable of achieving anything we set our minds to.

Chapter 5

The Road to Resilience

Building Inner Strength: Connect your growth in resilience to the disciplined focus and commitment to growth you nurtured.

My journey has been deeply influenced by Nicki Green. Finding a mentor like Nicki can be transformative. Look for someone who embodies where you want to be—whether they live in a house you admire, drive your dream car, or carry themselves in a manner you aspire to emulate. Engaging with such a person can provide invaluable insights into their mindset and behaviors. This is a glimpse into my relationship with Nicki, who has been a beacon of guidance in my life.

I met Nicki when I was in college. She had recently relocated to Chicago, Illinois, and had bought a piece of land to build her dream home. Over the years, our relationship evolved from a budding friendship into a robust mentorship. Nicki, who was several years my senior and had endured the loss of her son, became a cornerstone of support during my trials, especially when I had to attend monthly court hearings—Nicki understood well as she had faced similar challenges.

Our countless conversations, often during late work hours as I made up time lost to court visits, were filled with shared experiences and mutual support. Nicki's approach to life was straightforward, loving, and infinitely supportive. It's been over twenty-four years now, and I still turn to her for advice on everything from personal finance to family matters.

Nicki was instrumental during a critical financial decision in my life—refinancing my home. When I was considering pulling equity out of my home to pay off my car, she advised against extending the mortgage term to cover short-term gains, emphasizing the long-term financial impact. Her financial acumen was not just theoretical; she lived it, maintaining a lifestyle that was sustainable on a modest income, a testament to her savvy planning and disciplined budgeting.

Her support wasn't limited to financial advice. When I needed help navigating the educational system for my children, Nicki was there. She even accompanied me to school meetings, advocating on my behalf to ensure my children received the necessary resources. We have traveled halfway around the world together on a budget. We have been to places like Aruba, Budapest, Hawaii, Paris, just to name a few.

This profound relationship/mentorship has inspired me not just to survive, but to thrive. It underscores the power of having someone who believes in you, guides you, and challenges you to rise above your circumstances.

In memory of my daughter and influenced by the resilience and unwavering support of my mentor, I am committed to giving back. Through sharing my story and resources, I aim to support other single parents who are navigating their paths through hardship.

I encourage you to connect with mentors like Nicki, who can guide and inspire you. To further support single parents in building their support networks, I invite you to join our community at Help from a sister. Subscribe to our YouTube channel @helpfromasister and visit our website at www.helpfromasister.org. Here, you can share your experiences and learn from the journeys of others, enriching your path and possibly providing critical support to someone in need.

Finding Resilience Within: Exploring ways to tap into inner strength during tough times

When faced with challenging times, it's natural to feel overwhelmed and uncertain. The key is to remember that within you lies a well of resilience waiting to be tapped into. Think of resilience as your inner strength, ready to guide you through the storm. One way to connect with this resilience is by embracing self-compassion. Treat yourself with kindness and understanding, recognizing that you are doing the best you can in a difficult situation.

Another way to find resilience within is through mindfulness practices. Take a moment to breathe deeply and ground yourself in the present moment. This can help you gain perspective and clarity amid chaos. Reflect on past experiences where you have overcome adversity, drawing inspiration from your resilience. Remind yourself of your strengths and capabilities, knowing that you have the power to navigate through tough times.

Connecting with supportive relationships can also boost your resilience. Lean on loved ones for emotional support and encouragement. Sharing your struggles with others can help lighten the burden and remind you that you are not alone. Trust in the power of community to uplift and guide you through challenging moments.

Finally, remember that resilience is not about avoiding or ignoring adversity but rather facing it with courage and determination. Embrace the challenges before you as opportunities for growth and transformation. Know that each obstacle you overcome strengthens your resilience, equipping you for whatever may come your way. Trust in your inner strength, and you will weather the storm with grace and resilience.

Embracing Vulnerability: How being vulnerable can be a source of strength

Being vulnerable can be quite intimidating, right? It's like opening yourself up to potential hurt or rejection. But what if I told you that vulnerability is a source of strength? It's true. When you allow yourself to be vulnerable, you're showing courage and authenticity. You're being real and honest with yourself and others. And that takes inner strength.

Think about it, when you're vulnerable, you're allowing yourself to be seen and heard in your truest form. You're not hiding behind masks or walls. Instead, you're embracing your emotions and experiences, even the difficult ones. This openness can create deeper connections with others and lead to greater understanding and empathy.

Vulnerability also allows for growth and personal development. By acknowledging your vulnerabilities, you're acknowledging your humanity. You're recognizing that it's okay to not have all the answers or to have weaknesses. This acceptance can be incredibly empowering and liberating.

So, the next time you feel hesitant to show your vulnerable side, remember that it's not a sign of weakness. It's a sign of courage and strength. Embrace your vulnerabilities, lean into them, and watch how they can become sources of resilience and power in your life.

Cultivating a Positive Mindset: Strategies for maintaining a positive outlook in the face of adversity

When faced with challenges, it's easy to let negativity take over and cloud our judgment. However, maintaining a positive mindset can make a world of difference in how we navigate tough times. One powerful strategy is practicing gratitude. Taking the time to appreciate the good things in our lives, no matter how small, can shift our perspective and help us see the silver linings even in the darkest of clouds.

Another effective way to cultivate a positive mindset is through daily affirmations. Speaking kind and encouraging words to ourselves can boost our self-esteem and create a sense of optimism. Reminding ourselves of our strengths and capabilities can build resilience and help us tackle adversity with confidence.

Furthermore, staying present in the moment can also contribute to a positive outlook. By focusing on what we can control and letting go of worries about the past or future, we can reduce anxiety and increase our sense of peace. Mindfulness practices such as meditation or deep breathing exercises can help us stay grounded and centered, even in the face of challenges.

Lastly, surrounding ourselves with positive influences and supportive people can impact our mindset. Building a strong support system of friends, family, or mentors who uplift and encourage us can provide a valuable lifeline during difficult times. Their words of wisdom and empathy can help us see the light at the end of the tunnel and remind us that we are not alone in our struggles.

By incorporating these strategies into our daily lives, we can train our minds to see the positives amidst adversity, fostering a resilient and optimistic mindset that can carry us through even the toughest of times.

Seeking Support: The value of leaning on others for help and guidance during difficult times

When faced with challenges, it's natural to feel overwhelmed and alone. During these difficult times, seeking support from others can make a world of difference in navigating adversity. Whether it's a close friend, a family member, or a therapist, reaching out for help allows us to share our burdens and gain valuable insights from different perspectives.

Having a strong support system can provide comfort, encouragement, and practical assistance when we need it most. Just knowing that there are people who care about us and are willing to listen can alleviate feelings of isolation and despair. Sometimes, all it takes is a kind word or a listening ear to help us feel understood and supported.

Furthermore, seeking support during tough times can help us gain new insights and solutions to our problems. Others may offer fresh perspectives or share their own experiences of overcoming similar challenges, offering us hope and inspiration. By opening up and being vulnerable with others, we create space for connection and mutual understanding, strengthening our relationships in the process.

In addition, seeking professional support, such as therapy or counseling, can provide us with the tools and strategies needed to cope effectively with adversity. Therapists can offer guidance, validation, and practical skills to help us navigate through difficult emotions and situations. Sometimes, professional help can be the anchor that keeps us afloat during turbulent times.

Ultimately, leaning on others for support is not a sign of weakness but a courageous act of self-care. It takes strength to be vulnerable and reach out for help when we need it most. By surrounding ourselves with a supportive network of people who uplift and empower us, we can weather any storm with grace and resilience.

Learning from Setbacks: Reflecting on how setbacks can be opportunities for growth and learning

Setbacks can leave us feeling defeated and discouraged, but they also present valuable opportunities for growth and learning. When we face setbacks, it's easy to dwell on the negative aspects and see them as failures. However, reframing setbacks as steppingstones to success can shift our perspective.

Each setback offers a chance to reflect on what went wrong, what lessons can be learned, and how we can improve in the future. It's through these moments of adversity that we discover our resilience and strength. By embracing setbacks as learning experiences, we can turn them into catalysts for personal growth.

One way to learn from setbacks is to practice self-reflection. Taking the time to analyze the situation objectively and identify areas for improvement can lead to valuable insights. This introspective process allows us to not only acknowledge our mistakes but also understand the underlying factors that contributed to the setback.

Moreover, setbacks provide an opportunity to build resilience and develop coping mechanisms. By facing adversity and learning how to navigate challenges, we become better equipped to handle future setbacks with grace and determination. Adversity can be a powerful teacher, showing us our inner capabilities and pushing us to exceed our expectations.

It's important to remember that setbacks are not permanent roadblocks but temporary detours on the path to success. Viewing setbacks as opportunities for growth allows us to bounce back stronger and more determined than before. By embracing setbacks as part of the journey, we can transform them into valuable lessons that propel us forward towards our goals.

Practicing Self Compassion: Being kind to oneself during challenging times and recognizing one's own worth

Amidst the chaos and uncertainty of challenging times, it's easy to be hard on ourselves. We often criticize our actions, dwell on our mistakes, and hold ourselves to impossibly high standards. But what if, instead of being our own harshest critic, we choose to treat ourselves with kindness and compassion?

Practicing self-compassion is not a sign of weakness; rather, it is a powerful act of self-care. It means acknowledging our struggles and imperfections with empathy and understanding. Just as we would comfort a friend in need, we can offer the same compassion to ourselves.

During moments of turmoil and adversity, it's crucial to be gentle with ourselves. Instead of berating ourselves for our perceived shortcomings, we can choose to look at ourselves with a compassionate eye. This shift in perspective allows us to recognize our worth and value, even when the world around us may seem to be falling apart.

Self-compassion is not about ignoring our flaws or making excuses for our actions. Rather, it is about accepting ourselves unconditionally, flaws and all. By embracing our humanity, we can navigate challenging times with grace and resilience.

Amid adversity, practicing self-compassion can be a beacon of light, offering solace and comfort in the darkest of moments. It allows us to acknowledge our struggles without judgment and to extend the same kindness to ourselves that we would readily offer to others. By cultivating a sense of self-compassion, we can weather life's storms with a sense of inner strength and acceptance.

Adapting to Change: Discussing the importance of being flexible and adaptable in the face of adversity

My journey as a single parent has been complex and challenging, marked by my relationships with the fathers of my children, each unique and fraught with its own set of difficulties.

My first child's father didn't meet my son until he was four years old and even when he did, he couldn't maintain a stable relationship with him. When I inquired why it was so he admitted that he felt inadequate because I hadn't confronted him aggressively or reacted in any way to show I was hurt from what he did.

The father of my second child faced different challenges. He did not know how to be a father, which he attributed to his own father leaving when he was young.

After he married, his wife and he attempted to have my daughter spend Christmas with them. I was open to their involvement but requested they maintain her weekend activity schedule, which they found too burdensome. Furthermore, I wanted to ensure my daughter did not feel left out during familial celebrations like Christmas, which led to disagreements with his wife about how holidays should be spent. Eventually, I had to seek legal advice to resolve these issues effectively, always keeping my daughter's emotional well-being in mind.

Tragically, he later suffered an accident that took his sight, complicating his life significantly.

Throughout these experiences, I often reflected on the instrumental role my own father played in my life, something my children's fathers chose differently about. Learning that not all fathers will be the same, and sometimes external factors, like new partners, can influence a man's decisions about his children, was difficult but essential.

Being a single parent meant balancing multiple roles—working, schooling, and ensuring my children's well-being during some of our hardest times, including the painful months following my daughter's murder. Facing the court system, confronting the accused, and eventually finding it within myself to forgive him, were parts of my journey that tested and shaped me profoundly. Grief, with its unpredictable waves, has been a constant companion, reminding me of both my vulnerabilities and strengths.

This path has not only taught me about resilience and forgiveness but also about the importance of protecting and nurturing not just my children but also those around me. Life, with all its ups and downs, has taught me to adapt and protect, always striving to provide a safe and loving environment for my children to grow and flourish into the remarkable individuals they are destined to become.

Finding Purpose in Pain: Exploring how adversity can lead to personal growth and transformation

Adversity has a unique way of shaping us – sometimes in ways we never could have imagined. It's during the most trying times that we often find our deepest reservoirs of strength and resilience. The pain we experience can serve as a catalyst for profound personal growth and transformation.

When we are faced with challenges that push us to our limits, we have a choice – to succumb to the pain and let it consume us or to rise above it and emerge stronger on the other side. Adversity has a way of stripping away the superficial layers of our identity, revealing our core values and beliefs.

During pain and suffering, we are forced to confront uncomfortable truths about ourselves and the world around us. We are compelled to reevaluate our priorities, reassess our goals, and redefine our sense of purpose. Adversity forces us to dig deep within ourselves, tapping into reserves of courage and resilience we never knew we had.

Through the process of navigating through pain and adversity, we undergo a profound transformation. We shed old beliefs and limitations and emerge as more compassionate, empathetic, and understanding individuals. Adversity has a way of breaking down our walls, allowing us to connect more deeply with others and forge genuine, meaningful relationships.

In the crucible of suffering, we discover our inner reserves of strength and resilience. We learn that it is possible to find beauty in pain and that growth often emerges from the most unexpected places. Adversity, rather than being a source of despair, becomes a steppingstone towards personal evolution and self-discovery.

As we navigate through the dark tunnels of pain and adversity, we hold onto the glimmer of hope that lights our way. We realize that even in our darkest moments, there is a purpose to our suffering – a purpose that leads to growth, transformation, and a deeper understanding of ourselves and the world around us.

The Power of Hope: Highlighting the strength that comes from holding onto hope even in the darkest moments

Hope is a powerful force that can sustain us through the darkest moments. In times of adversity, it can be easy to feel overwhelmed and defeated. But holding onto hope can provide the strength and motivation needed to keep moving forward. Hope allows us to see beyond our current struggles and envision a brighter future. It gives us the courage to face challenges and the belief that better days are ahead.

Even when faced with obstacles, hope can help us persevere. It reminds us that difficult times are temporary and that we have the resilience to overcome them. By maintaining hope, we can stay focused on our goals and keep pushing forward despite setbacks. Hope is a beacon of light in the darkness, guiding us through the storm and reminding us that there is always a path forward.

In the face of adversity, hope can be a source of comfort and solace. It reminds us that we are not alone in our struggles and that things always can improve. Hope fuels our determination and inspires us to keep going, even when the road ahead seems uncertain. It gives us the strength to continue fighting for what we believe in and to never give up on our dreams.

The power of hope lies in its ability to transform our outlook on life. It allows us to embrace positivity and maintain a sense of optimism, no matter what challenges we may face. By holding onto hope, we can weather even the toughest storms and emerge stronger on the other side. Hope is not just a fleeting emotion – it is a mindset that can shape our actions and guide us toward a brighter future.

Chapter 6

Triumphs and Transformations

Reflecting on the moments when I achieved triumph felt overwhelming, yet incredibly empowering. Embracing freedom and personal growth played a pivotal role in these victories. Spiritual healing and letting go of past grievances opened up new possibilities for growth and self-discovery.

Challenging myself to expand and accelerate my growth journey was a self-help endeavor. The effort put into this journey yielded exponential growth and transformation, moving me from one stage to the next. Sharing insights and learning from others' experiences further enriched this process, highlighting unique paths to self-discovery.

Enlarging my faith and trusting in a higher power shifted my focus from fear and doubt to limitless possibilities. Reconnecting with my spiritual beliefs through prayer, fasting, and studying sacred texts brought clarity and strength to face challenges with unwavering faith. Exploring different resources and engaging in enlightening discussions with like-minded individuals broadened my spiritual perspective and deepened my connection to faith.

Personal Growth: Exploring how overcoming challenges has led to personal transformation and self-discovery

Through the journey of overcoming challenges, I have experienced profound personal growth that has reshaped my entire being. Each obstacle I faced served as a catalyst for transformation and self-discovery, pushing me to confront my fears and limitations. As I navigated through these difficult moments, I unearthed hidden strengths and capabilities within myself that I never knew existed.

The process of overcoming challenges forced me to reevaluate my beliefs, priorities, and perceptions. It encouraged me to venture beyond my comfort zone and explore uncharted territories of my potential. I learned to embrace vulnerability and uncertainty, realizing that true growth often emerges from moments of discomfort and adversity.

In the face of challenges, I discovered a newfound resilience and determination that propelled me forward with unwavering resolve. Each setback became an opportunity for introspection and growth, allowing me to cultivate a deeper sense of self-awareness and authenticity. Through this transformative journey, I learned to trust in my abilities and intuition, fostering a greater sense of confidence and empowerment.

Moreover, as I continued to overcome obstacles and setbacks, I cultivated a greater sense of empathy and compassion towards myself and others. I learned to approach challenges with a sense of curiosity and openness, viewing them as steppingstones toward personal growth rather than barriers. This shift in perspective enabled me to embrace the process of self-discovery with a spirit of curiosity and wonder, allowing me to uncover hidden facets of my identity and purpose.

Overall, the journey of overcoming challenges has been a profound and transformative experience, shaping me into a stronger, more resilient individual. It has propelled me towards a path of personal growth and self-discovery, reminding me of the limitless potential that lies within each of us, waiting to be unleashed through the trials and triumphs of life.

Finding Purpose: Uncovering the deeper meaning and significance behind the triumphs experienced

Through the challenges I faced and the triumphs I have achieved, I have come to realize that each victory holds a deeper significance. These moments of success are not just about overcoming obstacles; they are about uncovering a greater purpose in my journey. As I reflect on my experiences, I see how each triumph has been a steppingstone toward a clearer understanding of who I am and what I am meant to do.

There is a profound sense of fulfillment that comes from recognizing the deeper meaning behind my triumphs. It is not simply about reaching a goal or accomplishing a task; it is about aligning with my true purpose and living in alignment with my values and beliefs.

Each victory, no matter how big or small, serves as a reminder that I am on the right path and that my efforts are making a difference, not just for myself but for others as well.

In the moments of triumph, I find clarity and direction. The challenges I have overcome have shaped me into the person I am today, guiding me toward a greater understanding of my strengths, passions, and goals. Through these triumphs, I have gained a renewed sense of purpose and a deeper appreciation for the journey I am on.

As I continue to navigate the ups and downs of life, I hold onto the realization that each triumph is a testament to my resilience and determination. They remind me that I am capable of overcoming any obstacle that comes my way and that there is a greater purpose driving me forward. Each victory, no matter how hard-won, serves as a beacon of hope and inspiration, lighting the way toward a future filled with meaning and significance.

Embracing Change: Discussing how triumphs often bring about shifts in mindset and perspective

Triumphs have a way of propelling us into a new realm of possibilities. As we overcome challenges and achieve our goals, we are met with a shifting landscape of thoughts and beliefs. The very act of triumphing opens our minds to new perspectives and ways of thinking. We begin to see ourselves and the world around us in a different light.

Change becomes not only inevitable but welcomed with open arms. We embrace the evolution of our mindset and the transformative power of our experiences. The barriers that once held us back now seem insignificant in the face of our triumphs. We realize that there are endless opportunities for growth and expansion beyond our previous limitations.

With each triumph, we redefine our understanding of what is possible. Our perspective expands, allowing us to envision a future filled with even greater achievements. We learn to adapt to new circumstances and navigate challenges with confidence and resilience. The change that comes with triumph is not something to be feared but embraced as a natural part of our journey toward personal growth and fulfillment.

As our mindset shifts, so do our relationships with others. Our triumphs have a ripple effect, influencing and strengthening the connections we have with those around us. We inspire and uplift others with our stories of success, showing them that they too can overcome obstacles and achieve their dreams. Our relationships become infused with a newfound sense of trust and support, as we share in each other's victories and struggles.

Embracing change in the wake of triumph is a testament to our ability to adapt and grow. We learn to welcome the unknown and approach challenges with a sense of adventure and curiosity. Our viewpoint transforms, allowing us to see the beauty and potential in every situation. As we continue on our journey of personal growth, we carry with us the lessons learned from embracing change and the power of triumph to shape our lives for the better.

Impact on Relationships: Examining how personal triumphs can influence and strengthen connections with others

Personal triumphs have a ripple effect that extends far beyond ourselves. As we navigate and overcome challenges, our relationships with others are deeply impacted. These triumphs have the power to influence and strengthen the connections we have with those around us.

Our personal growth and transformations can inspire those closest to us. By demonstrating resilience and perseverance in the face of adversity, we show others that anything is possible with determination and a positive mindset. Our triumphs can serve as a beacon of hope for those going through their struggles, encouraging them to keep pushing forward.

Furthermore, triumphs can deepen our relationships with others. As we overcome obstacles and achieve our goals, we often rely on the support and encouragement of friends, family, and mentors. These shared experiences create a sense of camaraderie and trust that strengthens the bonds between us. Celebrating victories together fosters a sense of unity and collaboration that can endure even during challenging times.

The impact of personal triumphs on relationships goes beyond just the immediate circle of support. Our successes can also inspire others in our community or larger social networks. By sharing our stories of triumph, we can motivate and uplift those who may be facing their difficulties. In this way, personal triumphs have the power to create a ripple effect of positivity and growth that extends far beyond our own experiences.

The relationships we cultivate are integral to our journey of triumph and transformation. By recognizing and appreciating how our triumphs influence and strengthen these connections, we can continue to uplift and support one another on the path to success.

Overcoming Doubt: Confronting self-doubt and fears that may have hindered the path to success

Self-doubt can be a formidable obstacle on the path to success. It whispers in your ear, planting seeds of uncertainty and fear. It can make you question your abilities, your worth, and your dreams. However, overcoming doubt is a crucial step in achieving triumph. It requires facing those inner demons, acknowledging their presence, and then pushing past them.

One of the most powerful ways to combat self-doubt is by recognizing and celebrating your past triumphs. Remind yourself of the times you faced challenges and emerged victorious. Use those moments as fuel to propel you forward, knowing that you have overcome obstacles before and are capable of doing so again.

Another key strategy is to surround yourself with a supportive network of people who believe in you. Lean on your friends, family, mentors, and allies who can provide encouragement and remind you of your strengths when doubt creeps in. Their unwavering support can be the anchor that keeps you grounded as you navigate the uncertainties of your journey.

It's also important to practice compassion and kindness towards yourself. Treat yourself with the same level of understanding and forgiveness that you would offer to a friend facing similar doubts. Remember that it's okay to stumble, falter, and feel uncertain at times. What matters most is how you choose to respond to those feelings and move forward despite them.

Ultimately, overcoming doubt is a continuous process. It requires patience, perseverance, and a steadfast belief in yourself and your abilities. By confronting your fears and insecurities, you can break free from the constraints of self-doubt and pave the way for success and triumph in all aspects of your life.

Resilience and Persistence: Highlighting the importance of resilience and persisting through obstacles to achieve triumph

Resilience and persistence are like the unsung heroes of our journey, quietly working behind the scenes to propel us forward when doubt threatens to hold us back. They are the silent forces that keep us going, pushing us to persevere through challenges and setbacks.

In the face of obstacles and adversity, it is our resilience that allows us to bounce back, time and time again. It is the inner strength that helps us weather the storm, knowing that brighter days are ahead.

Persistence is the steady drumbeat that keeps us moving forward, one step at a time. It is the refusal to give up, even when the path ahead seems overwhelming and uncertain. It is the unwavering commitment to our goals that drives us to push through even when the going gets tough.

Together, resilience and persistence form a powerful duo, shaping our mindset and actions. They remind us that failure is not the end, but merely a steppingstone on the path to success. They teach us to adapt, learn, and grow from every experience, no matter how challenging it may be.

So, as we navigate the ups and downs of life, let us remember the importance of resilience and persistence. Let us embrace these qualities as our guiding lights, helping us navigate the twists and turns of our journey with courage and determination. Also, let us never forget that triumph is not merely about reaching the destination, but about the strength and resilience we exhibit along the way.

Redefining Success: Challenging conventional notions of success and embracing personal definitions of achievement

Success is often portrayed as reaching a certain milestone, achieving fame or fortune, or earning recognition from others. But what if success doesn't fit into this narrow box of expectations? What if success is not about external validation, but about internal growth and fulfillment? By redefining success, we have the power to break free from society's constraints and create our definition of achievement. Success can be found in small victories, moments of growth, and acts of kindness. It can be measured by the depth of our relationships, the impact we have on others, and the growth we experience along the way. When we challenge conventional notions of success, we open ourselves up to a world of possibilities and infinite potential. So, let's redefine success on our terms, embracing the unique journey that is ours to navigate.

Inspiring Others: Sharing stories of triumph to motivate and uplift those facing their challenges

As writers, we hold the power to inspire and uplift others through our stories of triumph. Our experiences can serve as beacons of hope for those facing their challenges, showing them that they are not alone in their struggles. Each victory, no matter how big or small, has the potential to resonate with someone who needs a glimmer of light in their darkness.

As I draft this book today, on April 27, 2024, I find myself reflecting on a particularly challenging week. April 21 marked the 26th year since my daughter's passing—a milestone that brings its own deep and complex emotions. Just a day later, on April 22, my mother confided in me her feelings of deep despair. She expressed a profound sense of weariness with life, telling me she no longer had the desire to eat, undergo therapy, or continue her struggle. Facing such a heartrending confession from my mother left me grappling with how to respond effectively and compassionately.

While processing this, on April 23, I received an unexpected call from my daughter's father. Despite the years and the distance between us, he reached out to check on her well-being, fully aware that she does not speak to him due to the strained nature of their relationship. During our conversation, he offered an apology for his shortcomings as a father and acknowledged the role I played in raising our daughter solo. He asked for my forgiveness—a gesture I accepted, believing deeply in the power of forgiveness, as I too seek it for my missteps. I told him that it was only by the grace of God that I managed to navigate the challenges of single parenthood.

The week's trials did not end there. Thursday, April 24, I received a call from a victim witness coordinator informing me that the person responsible for my daughter's murder had been released. Sharing these experiences in my book is not about boasting or suggesting that life simply happens around me rather than to me. It's about transparency and the raw, often painful reality of my journey. This narrative serves to illustrate the resilience required to face each day anew, amidst the ongoing challenges that life unceremoniously throws our way.

As we continue on our journey of personal development and self-discovery, let us remember the impact our words can have on others. Through the act of sharing our triumphs, we become beacons of inspiration, guiding others toward their moments of victory and transformation.

Continuing the Journey: Looking ahead to future triumphs and transformations, and the ongoing process of growth and development

In life, we are constantly evolving and growing, embracing new challenges and opportunities along the way. Each triumph we experience serves as a steppingstone to the next chapter of our story, pushing us to reach new heights and unlock our full potential. It's important to remember that the journey is ongoing, with no set destination in sight. We must continue to strive for personal growth and development, embracing change and facing adversity. The path ahead may be filled with unknown challenges, but with each triumph and transformation, we gain the strength and resilience needed to navigate whatever lies ahead. By staying true to ourselves and our values, we can shape our narrative and inspire others to do the same. So, let's continue this journey with courage and determination, ready to embrace whatever triumphs and transformations come our way, knowing that the best is yet to come.

Chapter 7

Lessons Learned and Shared

When it comes to supporting single parents, it truly does take a village. If you know a single parent, whether they are a man or a woman, and they have children of the opposite sex, consider stepping in to mentor or spend time with that child. Single parents do their utmost to raise well-rounded individuals, but children often seek validation and affirmation from the absent parent.

My daughter, once she was grown, confided in me about feeling neglected by her father and other male relatives who chose not to engage in her life. Single parents must reassure their children that such absences are not their fault. I've always told my children that if someone is meant to be in their life, they will be. However, this shouldn't deter them from striving to be the best they can be. Life can be overwhelming, and adults sometimes prioritize their challenges over the needs of others. Despite my own overwhelming experiences, I make it a point to reach out to others, do something nice, or simply check in. It helps me to step outside my struggles.

I've also had to explain to my children why they didn't receive many birthday gifts, despite us always bringing gifts to others' parties. I emphasized that it's not the responsibility of others to provide gifts; as their parent, that's my role. Yet, I understand the importance of gifts to a child's social experience and so, I started taking them on trips instead of throwing big parties. This not only saved money but also spared them the disappointment of unmet expectations at home parties.

Our first trip instead of a party was to Wisconsin Dells. My son, then five, and my daughter, three, enjoyed it, but my son later asked why he hadn't had a party like other kids. I realized then that no matter the experience, children still value traditional celebrations like cake and ice cream. So, I adjusted by combining travel with a small celebration to maintain those cherished traditions.

Following the philosophy of Dave Ramsey, "We live like no one else, so later we can live like no one else," I taught my children the value of sacrifice and planning. We agreed not to eat out for the first half of the year so we could afford our travel. This not only taught them budgeting and planning but also helped us enjoy richer experiences together.

From a young age, I involved my children in sports and other activities to ensure they had positive role models and structured schedules. This was especially important for exposing them to responsible adults who could offer different perspectives and support. My son and daughter were engaged in various sports and activities, which kept them busy and helped them develop diverse skills and interests.

Navigating these challenges as a single parent wasn't easy, but by including my children in the planning process and making strategic decisions, we managed to create a fulfilling and structured life. These experiences have taught us all invaluable life skills and brought us closer as a family. If you're a single parent, remember that involving your children in decisions and planning can be incredibly empowering for them and can help ease some of the burdens you carry.

Overcoming Obstacles with Resilience

Life is full of challenges, big and small. Some days, it feels like everything is going wrong, and it's hard to see a way out. But in those moments, when it seems like the world is against you, that's when resilience comes into play.

Resilience is like a muscle – the more you use it, the stronger it becomes. It's the ability to bounce back from setbacks, face adversity, and come out on the other side stronger than before. It's not about ignoring the obstacles in your path, but about facing them with courage and determination.

When faced with obstacles, it's important to remember that you have the power to overcome them. It's not always easy, and there will be times when you want to give up. But that's when you dig deep and find that inner strength to keep going.

Resilience is also about being flexible and adaptable. Sometimes, the road to success is not a straight line – there will be twists and turns along the way. And that's okay. Embrace the challenges and see them as opportunities for growth and learning.

Remember, it's okay to ask for help when you need it. You don't have to face challenges alone. Reach out to friends, family, or a mentor for support and guidance. Sometimes, a different perspective can make all the difference in how you approach obstacles.

So, when life throws obstacles your way, remember that you have the power to overcome them. Stay strong, stay resilient, and keep moving forward.

Finding Silver Linings in Challenges

Life is full of challenges, each one bringing its own set of obstacles and struggles. But amidst these trials, there is often a glimmer of hope, a silver lining waiting to be discovered. It's all about perspective, about shifting our focus from the darkness of the challenge to the light of possibility.

When faced with adversity, it can be easy to get lost in negativity and to feel overwhelmed by the weight of the situation. But what if we choose to see challenges as opportunities for growth? What if we view setbacks as steppingstones to something bigger and better?

Finding silver linings in challenges requires us to change our mindset, to approach difficulties with a sense of curiosity and openness. Instead of dwelling on what went wrong, we can start looking for lessons learned, for hidden blessings in disguise. It's about recognizing that even in our darkest moments, there is still a glimmer of hope shining through.

By embracing the idea of finding silver linings, we can start to see challenges as catalysts for positive change. We can begin to appreciate the strength and resilience we possess, knowing that each obstacle we overcome only makes us stronger. And most importantly, we can cultivate a sense of gratitude for the lessons learned along the way.

So, the next time life throws a curveball your way, remember to look for the silver linings. Embrace the challenge with an open heart and a curious mind, knowing that within every storm lies the potential for growth and transformation.

Cultivating Self Compassion

Cultivating self-compassion is a gentle, yet powerful practice that can transform the way we relate to ourselves. It involves treating ourselves with kindness, understanding, and acceptance, especially in times of difficulty or struggle. Instead of being our own harshest critic, we become our own best ally, offering comfort and support when we need it most. Self-compassion allows us to acknowledge our imperfections and mistakes without judgment, recognizing that we are all human and deserving of love and compassion, including ourselves. It helps us to build resilience and inner strength, fostering a sense of security and self-worth that is not dependent on external validation. By cultivating self-compassion, we learn to be kinder to ourselves, to embrace our vulnerabilities and imperfections, and to treat ourselves with the same care and compassion that we would offer to a dear friend in need.

Embracing Vulnerability for Growth

Vulnerability is often seen as a weakness, something to be avoided at all costs. But what if we flipped that narrative? What if we viewed vulnerability as a powerful tool for growth and self-discovery? Embracing vulnerability means being willing to show up, fully and authentically, even when it's uncomfortable. It requires courage to be open and honest about our fears, insecurities, and struggles.

When we allow ourselves to be vulnerable, we create space for true connection with others. We let down our walls and invite others in, fostering deeper relationships built on trust and authenticity. Vulnerability also opens the door to growth and self-improvement. By acknowledging our vulnerabilities and facing them, we can learn valuable lessons about ourselves and our capabilities.

It's important to remember that vulnerability is not synonymous with weakness. It takes great strength to be vulnerable, confront our fears, and expose our true selves to the world. By embracing vulnerability, we can unlock new levels of personal growth and resilience. So, let's embrace our vulnerabilities, lean into discomfort, and watch ourselves grow in ways we never thought possible.

Navigating Change with Grace

Navigating change with grace requires a willingness to let go of old ways of being and embracing the unknown with an open heart. Change can be scary and unsettling, but it also offers us the opportunity to grow and evolve. It's important to remember that change is a natural part of life, and resisting it only causes more suffering. Instead, try to approach change with curiosity and a sense of adventure.

When faced with a major life change, it's normal to feel a range of emotions, from fear and uncertainty to excitement and hope. Allow yourself to feel these emotions without judgment, knowing that they are all part of the process. Take some time to reflect on how this change is impacting you and what it means for your future. By acknowledging your feelings and thoughts, you can begin to make sense of the situation and find a way forward.

As you navigate through change, remember to be kind to yourself. Give yourself permission to take things one step at a time and be patient with yourself during this transition. It's okay to feel overwhelmed or unsure of what to do next. Trust that you have the strength and resilience to weather this storm and come out stronger on the other side.

Practice self-care during times of change by prioritizing activities that nourish your body, mind, and soul. This could include spending time in nature, meditating, journaling, or seeking support from loved ones. Remember that self-care looks different for everyone, so find what works best for you and make it a priority.

Lastly, stay open to the possibilities that change brings. Instead of clinging to the past or worrying about the future, focus on being present in the moment and embracing the opportunities that come your way. Change can be a doorway to new beginnings and growth, and by navigating it with grace, you can emerge stronger and more resilient than ever before.

Harnessing the Power of Mindfulness

Mindfulness is the practice of being fully present and aware of the current moment. It involves paying attention to our thoughts, feelings, and sensations without judgment. When we harness the power of mindfulness, we can navigate life's challenges with greater ease and clarity. By taking the time to pause, breathe, and tune into our inner selves, we can cultivate a sense of peace and tranquility amidst the chaos of change. Mindfulness allows us to observe our thoughts and emotions without getting caught up in them, fostering a sense of detachment and perspective. Through mindfulness, we can become more attuned to our inner guidance and intuition, helping us make decisions that align with our true values and goals. By practicing mindfulness regularly, we can cultivate a sense of inner calm and resilience that sustains us through life's ups and downs.

Embracing Imperfection and Authenticity

Embracing imperfection can be a liberating experience. It's about letting go of the unrealistic expectations we set for ourselves and accepting that we are not flawless beings. Authenticity comes from being true to ourselves, flaws, and all. When we embrace our imperfections, we are free to show up as our genuine selves without the fear of judgment. By being authentic, we allow others to see the real person behind the facade. It creates deeper connections and fosters genuine relationships based on trust and mutual understanding. Imperfection is what makes us human, and it's through our imperfections that we can truly connect with others on a deeper level.

So, embrace your imperfections, for they are what make you uniquely you.

Cultivating Empathy and Connection

Empathy is a powerful tool that allows us to connect with others on a deeper level. It involves putting ourselves in someone else's shoes and understanding their perspective, even if we may not agree with it. By cultivating empathy, we open ourselves up to a world of understanding and compassion.

Connection is a fundamental human need. We thrive on meaningful relationships and interactions with others. When we cultivate empathy, we not only enhance our ability to understand others but also strengthen our connections with them. It creates a sense of shared humanity and builds trust and rapport.

Empathy and connection go hand in hand. They form the foundation of positive relationships and allow us to bridge gaps in understanding. By practicing empathy in our interactions, we can create a more compassionate and connected world.

In our journey of personal growth and self-discovery, cultivating empathy and connection is essential. It helps us break down barriers, foster understanding, and create a sense of unity with those around us. As we extend kindness and compassion to others, we also nurture our sense of empathy and deepen our connections with the world.

Paying it Forward: Sharing Wisdom with Others

As we journey through life and gather our own experiences and lessons, it becomes our privilege and responsibility to share that wisdom with others. There is immense power in paying it forward, in being the light that guides someone through their darkness. When we share our knowledge, struggles, and triumphs, we create a ripple effect of inspiration and growth.

Sharing wisdom with others is not just about imparting knowledge; it's about building connections and fostering empathy. It's about showing others that they are not alone in their journey and that we have all faced challenges and setbacks. By sharing our stories, we offer hope and comfort to those who may be struggling.

Each interaction, no matter how small, is an opportunity to make a positive impact on someone else's life. Whether it's lending a listening ear, offering advice, or simply being present, we have the power to uplift and empower those around us. In doing so, we not only help others navigate their paths, but we also strengthen our sense of purpose and fulfillment.

Paying it forward is a continuous cycle of giving and receiving, of learning and teaching. It's about creating a community of support and understanding were kindness and empathy reign supreme. As we share our wisdom with others, we create a bond that transcends words and actions, a bond that speaks to the interconnectedness of all humanity.

So let us embrace the opportunity to pay it forward, to share our wisdom and our kindness with others. Let us be beacons of light in a world that can often seem dark and uncertain. Also, let us remember that by sharing our wisdom, we not only enrich the lives of others, but we also enrich our souls.

Chapter 8

Building a Supportive Community

As we navigate through the tapestry of our lives, we often realize the profound impact that community has on our journey. Our community shapes our experiences, perspectives, and our sense of belonging. But what exactly is a community? It's more than just a group of people living in the same area or sharing common interests. A community is a supportive network that provides us with connections, relationships, and a sense of unity. It's a place where we can be ourselves, feel understood, and find comfort in times of need. In this chapter, we will delve into the importance of community and explore how finding our tribe can enrich our lives in ways we never thought possible.

Finding Your Tribe the Importance of Community

Have you ever felt like you're on your little island, navigating the twists and turns of life all by yourself? It's a tough road to travel, so why not find your tribe?

Think of your tribe as your squad, your crew, or your people. These are the ones who understand you, support you, and lift you when you're down. Finding your tribe is like discovering your home away from home—a place where you can truly be yourself without fear of judgment.

Your tribe consists of those who share your values, your interests, and your passions. These are the people who will celebrate your successes with genuine joy and offer a shoulder to lean on during tough times. They are your cheerleaders, your confidants, your partners in crime.

Building a supportive community isn't just about having people around—it's about surrounding yourself with those who truly care about your well-being. These are the friends who will check in on you when you're feeling low, encourage you to chase your dreams, and challenge you to be the best version of yourself.

In a world that can sometimes feel cold and impersonal, your tribe is the warm hug that reminds you that you are never alone. So, don't hesitate to reach out, connect, or find your people. Your tribe is out there waiting for you, ready to welcome you with open arms.

To further support single parents in finding and building their tribes, I invite you to join our community, Help from a sister. We're here to offer the essential support and understanding that every single parent needs. You can become a part of our journey by subscribing to our YouTube channel @helpfromasister and visiting our website at https://www.helpfromasister.org. Here, you can share your stories, learn from others, and find resources that can make a real difference in your life.

Let's build this supportive community together. Your story is powerful, and your experiences can inspire and uplift others. Share your journey, join the conversation, and help us spread kindness and support across our network. Together, we can ensure that no single parent has to navigate this path alone.

Nurturing Relationships Cultivating Connections

Building and maintaining relationships is a fundamental part of building a supportive community. It's about more than just networking, it's about cultivating genuine connections with people who care about your wellbeing. Take the time to invest in these relationships, nurturing them with kindness, respect, and understanding. Whether it's through shared experiences, conversations, or simple acts of kindness, each interaction has the potential to strengthen the bond between individuals. By fostering these connections, you create a sense of belonging and trust within your community. So, don't underestimate the power of a kind word, a listening ear, or a helping hand in nurturing relationships that will enrich your life and those around you.

Shared Goals and Values Uniting for a Common Purpose

Imagine a gathering of individuals, each with their unique backgrounds, experiences, and perspectives coming together under a shared vision. This is the essence of uniting for a common purpose. When we align our goals and values towards a collective mission, the possibilities are limitless.

In this space of collaboration, we find strength in unity. By recognizing that our objectives can merge harmoniously with the aspirations of others, we create a powerful constructive collaboration that propels us forward. It is through this alignment that we discover the deeper meaning behind our pursuits and the impact we can have when we work together towards a shared goal.

As we navigate the intricacies of our common purpose, we learn to appreciate the diversity of ideas and approaches that each person brings to the table. By honoring and respecting these differences, we not only enrich our collective experience but also broaden our perspectives, enabling us to explore new horizons and innovate in ways we never thought possible.

Through the lens of shared goals and values, we foster a sense of belonging and camaraderie that transcends individual ambitions. As we celebrate each other's successes and support one another in times of challenge, we build a strong foundation of trust and mutual respect that strengthens our bond and fuels our collective progress.

In this journey towards a common purpose, we are reminded that our differences do not divide us but instead serve as the threads that weave together the fabric of our community. It is through this tapestry of shared goals and values that we find meaning, purpose, and a sense of belonging that propels us towards a brighter future, united in our quest for growth and fulfillment.

Diversity and Inclusion Embracing Differences

Diversity is like a colorful tapestry, woven together by different threads that create a beautiful and intricate pattern. In our community, we celebrate these differences, recognizing that each individual brings a unique perspective and set of experiences to the table. Whether it's our various cultural backgrounds, beliefs, or ways of thinking, we understand that diversity is a strength, not a weakness.

Embracing these differences allows us to learn from one another, broaden our horizons, and challenge our own biases and assumptions. By listening to each other's stories, we gain a deeper understanding of the world around us and develop empathy and compassion for those who may have walked a different path than our own.

Inclusion is the key to unlocking the full potential of our community. It's about creating a space where everyone feels welcomed, valued, and respected for who they are. When we embrace diversity and foster a culture of inclusivity, we tap into the collective wisdom and creativity of all individuals, regardless of their background or identity.

By coming together in unity, with shared goals and values, and by building supportive networks that act as safety nets for one another, we create a foundation that is strong and resilient. But it is through embracing our differences, through actively seeking out diverse perspectives and voices, that we truly enrich our community and propel it towards greater heights.

So let us continue to welcome diversity with open arms, celebrate the unique qualities that make each of us who we are, and work together towards a future that is inclusive, equitable, and full of endless possibilities.

Supportive Networks Creating a Safety Net

Supportive networks are like a safety net that we all need on our journey. They provide a sense of security and comfort, knowing that there are people who have your back no matter what. These networks can consist of friends, family, mentors, colleagues, or even online communities.

When you have a supportive network, you feel empowered to take risks and step out of your comfort zone. You know that people are rooting for you and ready to offer guidance or assistance when needed.

Building these connections takes time and effort, but the payoff is immense.

In a supportive network, you can freely express your thoughts and emotions without fear of judgment. You can be vulnerable and authentic, knowing that you are accepted for who you are. This level of acceptance fosters a sense of belonging and strengthens your resilience in facing challenges.

These networks also offer valuable resources and perspectives that can enrich your journey. By connecting with individuals from diverse backgrounds and experiences, you gain new insights and ideas that you may not have considered on your own. Collaboration and cooperation thrive in such a nurturing environment.

Moreover, supportive networks provide a safe space to receive constructive feedback and guidance. This feedback is essential for personal growth and improvement. It helps you learn from your mistakes and continuously evolve as a person and a professional.

In times of distress or uncertainty, your supportive network acts as a source of comfort and reassurance. Whether you need a listening ear, a helping hand, or just a shoulder to lean on, knowing that you have a supportive community to turn to can make all the difference.

As you cultivate and nurture your supportive network, remember that it is a two-way street. Be willing to offer support and encouragement to others in return. Building a strong community is a collaborative effort, and by lifting each other, we create a network that is truly a safety net for all its members.

Collaboration and Cooperation Strength in Numbers

Imagine a world where everyone works together, where collaboration and cooperation are the norm. In this world, individuals come together, pooling their resources and talents to achieve common goals. There is strength in numbers, they say, and it couldn't be truer. When people unite, amazing things can happen.

Picture a community where each person brings something unique to the table. Different backgrounds, skills, and perspectives blend seamlessly, creating a tapestry of diversity that enriches everyone involved. By working together, they can tackle challenges that might seem insuperable on their own.

Collaboration is not just about achieving a goal; it's about building relationships and trust. When people come together to collaborate, they must communicate openly and honestly, listen to each other's ideas, and be willing to compromise. It's a give-and-take, a dance of cooperation that requires mutual respect and understanding.

Cooperation is the glue that holds a collaborative effort together. It's about setting ego aside and personal agendas for the greater good. When individuals cooperate, they contribute their strengths while also being willing to support others in their areas of weakness. It's a symbiotic relationship where each person plays a vital role in the success of the collective endeavor.

In a world that often emphasizes individual achievement, collaboration, and cooperation remind us of the power of working together. When we join forces, we amplify our impact, create lasting change, and build a more connected and resilient community. Strength truly lies in numbers when we come together with a spirit of collaboration and cooperation.

Giving Back: The Power of Generosity

Generosity is a powerful force that can transform not only the lives of others but also our own. When we give back to our community, whether through acts of kindness, donations, or volunteering, we are not only helping those in need but also creating a ripple effect of positivity and goodwill.

It's through giving that we can truly make a difference in the world. By sharing our time, resources, and skills with others, we uplift those around us and create a sense of unity and connection. The act of generosity does not have to be grand or extravagant, even the smallest gestures can have a profound impact on someone's life.

Help From A Sister Inc. Empowering Communities Through Compassionate Initiatives

Our organization is dedicated to uplifting underprivileged communities through a variety of impactful initiatives and grassroots efforts. Since 2020, we have consistently worked towards making a positive difference, with a strong focus on education, providing sustenance, and fostering community connections.

Key Achievements:

2020: Assisted 250 homeless individuals with meals and care packets; supported families with cash donations.

2021: Awarded 10 gifts to graduating students; donated bookbags filled with school supplies to 250 students.

2022: Organized fun events for 25 children, including a circus trip; executed a large gift card and toy giveaway. Donated 500 bookbags filled with school supplies.

2023: Donated 1,000 bookbags filled with school supplies; adopted Caldwell Elementary in Chicago; hosted weekly food giveaways; launched a community-focused podcast; held monthly networking meetings; conducted a massive toy giveaway for 250 children.

2024: Continuation of food giveaways and networking meetings; planned a Single Parent Empowerment Conference, donating 1,000 book bags filled with supplies, we have taken 40 children to the circus, a Thanksgiving turkey giveaway for 250 single parents, and a holiday toy distribution for 300 children.

Our mission is to empower single parents by equipping them with the knowledge and tools necessary to increase their income streams and achieve financial stability. As a single parent, I understand the importance of finding reliable resources and creating opportunities for financial growth. Welcome to our service dedicated to assisting single parents, led by a fellow single parent, in discovering strategies to generate additional income and find valuable resources. We understand the challenges that single parents face firsthand, and we're here to provide guidance and support every step of the way.

Let us embrace the power of generosity and make a commitment to give back to our community, knowing that together, we can create a world filled with kindness, compassion, and hope.

Overcoming Challenges Together Weathering Storms

When we face challenges in life, it can feel like we're battling against the wind, struggling to stay afloat in turbulent waters. These storms can be overwhelming, leaving us feeling helpless and alone. But there is strength in numbers, and when we come together as a community, we can weather these storms with courage and resilience.

As we face challenges together, we offer each other a shoulder to lean on, a listening ear, and a comforting presence. We share our struggles and fears, knowing that we are not alone in our journey. In this shared vulnerability, we find strength in our solidarity and unity.

Through collaboration and cooperation, we pool our resources and talents to navigate through the darkest moments. We offer support and guidance, lifting each other when we feel weary and worn down. Together, we can overcome even the toughest obstacles that life throws our way.

In times of struggle, it is essential to lean on one another for support. We remind each other of our resilience and inner strength, encouraging one another to keep pushing forward, even when the road ahead seems steep and treacherous. Together, we can find the courage to face our challenges, knowing that we have a community that stands beside us, ready to catch us if we stumble.

As we weather these storms together, we forge unbreakable bonds, rooted in empathy, compassion, and mutual understanding. Our shared experiences bind us together, creating a tapestry of resilience and unity that can withstand any adversity. In overcoming challenges together, we not only survive but thrive, emerging stronger and more united than ever before.

Celebrating Success, The Joy of Achieving Together

After overcoming challenges together, it's time to bask in the glow of our collective success. The joy of achieving together is unlike anything else. It's not just about individual victories; it's about the shared journey and the bonds we've formed along the way.

As we celebrate our successes, let's take a moment to recognize the hard work and dedication that got us here. Each milestone reached is a testament to our collective strength and determination. And it's not just about reaching the destination; it's about savoring the moments of progress and growth that we experienced together.

Whether it's a small win or a major accomplishment, every success deserves to be acknowledged and celebrated. So, let's raise a glass, pat each other on the back, and revel in the joy of our achievements. Let's share stories, laughter, and memories that will forever bind us together as a supportive community.

In this moment of celebration, let's not forget to express gratitude to those who stood by us, supported us, and believed in us when times were tough. Our success is not just our own; it belongs to everyone who contributed to our journey in their unique way. Together, we are stronger, more resilient, and capable of achieving great things.

Here's to-us to the moments of struggle that made us stronger, to the triumphs that brought us closer, and to the joy of achieving together. Let's continue to support and uplift each other as we navigate future challenges and celebrate many more successes to come.

Chapter 9

Continuing the Journey

As you look back on your journey, it's important to recognize the growth you've experienced and the progress you've made. Through the guidance of this book, you have witnessed firsthand the transformation that is possible when you commit to self-improvement and resilience. Reflect on the challenges you have overcome, the lessons you have learned, and the person you have become along the way.

Now is the time to take the next step in your journey. Consider setting new goals that align with your values and aspirations. What dreams would you pursue if you believed that your positive thoughts could turn them into reality? Embrace the potential for growth and change as you continue on your path of personal development.

I encourage you to embark on or persist in your journey of self-improvement and resilience. Remember that progress is not always linear, and setbacks may occur. Stay committed to your goals, seek support from your community, and draw strength from within.

I express my gratitude to you, the reader, for engaging in this journey of reflection and growth. Your dedication to self-improvement is commendable, and I look forward to witnessing the positive transformations that lie ahead for you. Trust in your potential, believe in your abilities and embrace the challenges that come your way. Your journey is unique, and the possibilities for growth are endless.

Setting New Goals: Exploring the next steps in your journey

As you reflect on how far you've come, it's only natural to start thinking about what lies ahead. Setting new goals is an exciting and important part of your journey. It's a chance to challenge yourself, push your boundaries, and continue growing in ways you never imagined.

Consider where you are now and where you want to be in the future. What do you want to achieve? What dreams and aspirations do you still hold dear? Take the time to visualize your goals clearly, allowing yourself to dream big and reach for the stars.

Remember, setting new goals is not just about the destination but the journey itself. Embrace the process of growth and transformation that comes with working towards your goals. Be open to new experiences, new ideas, and new opportunities that may come your way.

Stay flexible and adaptable as you navigate the twists and turns of your journey. Embrace change as a natural part of life and a chance to learn and grow. Be willing to step out of your comfort zone and challenge yourself in new ways.

Believe in yourself and your ability to achieve your goals. Trust in your inner strength and resilience. With determination, hard work, and a positive mindset, you can reach new heights and create a future that is truly fulfilling and rewarding.

So, go ahead and set those new goals. Embrace the challenges and opportunities that lie ahead. Your journey is just beginning, and the possibilities are endless.

Embracing Change: Adapting to new challenges and opportunities

Change can be overwhelming, but it also brings new possibilities and chances for growth. Embracing change means being open to the unknown and being willing to step outside your comfort zone. It's about being flexible and adaptable in the face of new challenges and opportunities.

When faced with change, it's important to approach it with a positive mindset. Rather than seeing it as a threat, view it as a chance to learn and evolve. Change can push you to discover new strengths and capabilities you never knew you had.

One way to embrace change is to stay curious and open-minded. Be willing to explore different perspectives and approaches and be open to trying new things. By staying flexible and willing to adapt, you can navigate change with more ease and grace.

Remember that change is a natural part of life, and resisting it only hinders your growth. Instead of fearing change, see it as a chance to reinvent yourself and your life. Embrace the unknown, seize new opportunities, and trust in your ability to navigate whatever comes your way.

Finding Inspiration: Seeking motivation to keep moving forward

In life's journey, there are moments when we may feel stuck or unsure of our next steps. It is during these times that finding inspiration becomes crucial in helping us stay motivated and keep moving forward. Inspiration can come from various sources, whether it's a quote that resonates with you, a story of someone overcoming adversity, or simply the beauty of nature around you.

One powerful way to find inspiration is by connecting with others who share similar goals and dreams. Surrounding yourself with positive and motivated individuals can fuel your drive and determination. Sharing ideas, experiences, and even setbacks with like-minded people can offer fresh perspectives and spark new ideas.

Another way to tap into inspiration is by exposing yourself to new experiences and challenges. Stepping out of your comfort zone and trying new things can ignite a sense of excitement and possibility.

Whether it's traveling to a new place, learning a new skill, or taking on a new project, embracing change and seeking out opportunities can open up a world of inspiration.

Reflecting on your past achievements and how far you've come can also serve as a powerful source of motivation. Reminding yourself of the obstacles you've overcome and the progress you've made can reignite your passion and determination to continue pushing forward. Celebrate your successes, no matter how small, and use them as steppingstones to propel you toward your next goal.

Lastly, remember to nurture your well-being. Prioritizing self-care is essential in maintaining the energy and motivation needed to pursue your dreams. Taking time to rest, recharge, and engage in activities that bring you joy, and fulfillment can help you stay inspired and focused on your journey. Remember, finding inspiration is a continuous process, so stay open to new possibilities and keep seeking out sources of motivation to fuel your path forward.

Nurturing Self-care: Prioritizing your well-being along the way

Nurturing self-care is a vital aspect of any journey toward personal growth and fulfillment. It involves taking the time to prioritize your well-being and make choices that support your physical, mental, and emotional health. Self-care is not selfish; it is a necessary practice that allows you to show up as your best self in all areas of your life.

Self-care looks different for everyone, as it is deeply personal and unique to each individual. It can include activities such as exercise, meditation, journaling, spending time in nature, or indulging in a hobby that brings you joy. Remember, self-care isn't about bubble baths and massages; it's about tuning into your needs and taking intentional steps to nurture yourself.

Listen to your body and mind, and honor what they are telling you. If you are feeling overwhelmed or stressed, give yourself permission to rest and recharge. Set boundaries that protect your time and energy, saying no to things that drain you and yes to activities that fuel your spirit. Prioritize sleep, nutrition, and hydration, recognizing that your physical well-being directly impacts your mental and emotional state.

Practice mindfulness and self-compassion, offering yourself grace and understanding when things don't go as planned. Be kind to yourself, just as you would be to a friend in need. Take breaks when you need them and cultivate a sense of balance in your life that allows you to thrive.

Self-care is an ongoing practice, not a one-time event. It requires commitment and consistency to make it a priority in your daily routine. By nurturing yourself with kindness and compassion, you are investing in your overall well-being and creating a foundation for continued growth and resilience.

Seeking Support: Utilizing your community for guidance and encouragement

It's essential to remember that you don't have to navigate your journey alone. Seeking support from your community can provide you with the guidance and encouragement you need to keep moving forward. Your community consists of people who care about you, want to see you succeed, and are ready to offer a helping hand when you need it most. Whether it's friends, family, mentors, or colleagues, reaching out for support can make a world of difference in how you approach challenges and celebrate successes.

Don't hesitate to lean on your community for advice and perspective, as they can offer valuable insights and a different way of looking at things. Engaging with others can lead to new ideas, solutions, and opportunities that you might not have considered on your own. By opening up to those around you, you create space for collaboration and growth, allowing you to tap into a wealth of knowledge and experiences that can help you overcome obstacles and achieve your goals.

Remember that asking for support is a sign of strength, not weakness. It shows that you are willing to be vulnerable and acknowledge that you can't do everything on your own. Building a support system of trusted individuals who believe in you and your abilities can boost your confidence and motivation, providing you with the encouragement and reassurance you need to push through tough times and celebrate your accomplishments.

So, don't be afraid to reach out and connect with your community. Whether it's sharing your challenges, seeking advice, or simply celebrating your wins, involving others in your journey can enhance your overall experience and make the road ahead more fulfilling and rewarding. Your community is there to cheer you on, lift you, and remind you that you are capable of achieving great things.

Milestones and Turning Points: Realizing My Strength

Through the highs and lows of life, I have encountered numerous milestones and turning points that have shaped me into the person I am today. These moments of victory and challenges have allowed me to tap into reserves of strength I never knew I possessed. A pivotal moment was overcoming a personal crisis that threatened to break me. It was during this time that I realized the depth of my resilience and inner fortitude. The ability to rise above adversity and come out stronger on the other side was a testament to my unwavering spirit and determination.

Transitioning to a new phase in my career was also a significant turning point. Stepping out of my comfort zone and taking on new challenges forced me to confront my fears and push past self-imposed limitations. It was a transformative experience that allowed me to expand my horizons and explore uncharted territories.

Moreover, the relationships I have cultivated along the way have also been instrumental in my journey of self-discovery. The unwavering support and encouragement from loved ones have served as pillars of strength during times of doubt and uncertainty. Their belief in me has been a constant source of motivation, reminding me of the power of community and connection.

Reflecting on these milestones and turning points, I am filled with a sense of gratitude for the journey that has brought me to where I am today. Each obstacle overcome, each triumph celebrated, has contributed to the tapestry of my life, painting a picture of resilience, growth, and endless possibility.

Celebrating Milestones: Recognizing and appreciating your achievements

It's time to celebrate! Take a moment to reflect on how far you've come. Think back to all the challenges you've faced and overcome. Those moments of doubt and uncertainty that you pushed through with determination and resilience.

Remember the times when you wanted to give up but didn't? Acknowledge the hard work and dedication you've put into reaching this point. Whether big or small, each milestone deserves recognition.

It could be you finally finishing that project you've been working on for months. Or stepping out of your comfort zone and trying something new. Whatever it is, give yourself credit for the progress you've made.

Celebrate your achievements with those who have supported you along the way. Share your successes with friends, family, or mentors who have been there to cheer you on. Let them share in your joy and revel in your accomplishments.

Be proud of yourself and the journey you've embarked on. Celebrate the milestones, no matter how small they may seem. Each step forward is a victory worth celebrating. So, take a moment to pat yourself on the back and bask in the glow of your achievements. You've earned it.

Overcoming Setbacks: Dealing with setbacks and learning from them

Setbacks will inevitably come our way, challenging our perseverance and resilience. Whether it's a rejection letter, a project that doesn't go as planned, or personal struggles that weigh us down, setbacks can be tough to navigate. However, it's important to remember that setbacks are not roadblocks but rather detours on our journey towards growth and success.

When faced with a setback, it's natural to feel disappointed, frustrated, or even defeated. These emotions are valid, but it's crucial not to dwell on them for too long. Instead, acknowledge your feelings, process them, and then shift your focus towards finding solutions and lessons to be learned from the setback.

One way to overcome setbacks is to reframe them as opportunities for growth and learning. Reflect on what went wrong, what factors were within your control, and what you can do differently next time. Every setback is a chance to reassess your goals, strategies, and mindset, leading to a stronger, wiser version of yourself.

Seek support from your community during challenging times. Share your setbacks with trusted friends, mentors, or colleagues who can offer guidance, perspective, and encouragement. Remember that you are not alone in facing setbacks, and others may have valuable insights to share that can help you navigate through tough times.

It's important to practice self-compassion during setbacks. Be kind to yourself and avoid self-criticism or negative self-talk. Remember that setbacks are a natural part of any journey, and they do not define your worth or capabilities. Treat yourself with the same level of respect and understanding that you would offer to a friend facing a similar situation.

Setbacks are temporary obstacles that can be overcome with time, patience, and resilience. Stay focused on your long-term goals and vision and use setbacks as steppingstones towards your ultimate success. By embracing setbacks as opportunities for growth and learning, you'll emerge stronger, more resilient, and better equipped to manage whatever challenges come your way in the future.

Staying Resilient: Cultivating the strength to persevere through tough times

During challenging times, it's important to remember that resilience comes from within. It's not about avoiding setbacks, but about how we respond to them. When faced with adversity, our ability to stay resilient can make all the difference. Cultivating strength in the face of tough times allows us to weather the storm and emerge even stronger on the other side.

Resilience is like a muscle that gets stronger with each setback we overcome. It's about-facing difficulties, learning from them, and using those lessons to propel us forward. It's understood that setbacks are not the end of the road but merely detours along the way.

In times of struggle, it's natural to feel overwhelmed, frustrated, or even defeated. But it's in these moments that our resilience is evaluated and forged. By reminding ourselves of past challenges we have overcome, we can draw upon that inner strength to push through the toughest of times.

Staying resilient also involves seeking support from others. Surrounding ourselves with a supportive community can provide comfort, encouragement, and a different perspective on the situation. It's okay to lean on others for help when needed, as it takes strength to admit when we need support.

Above all, staying resilient means having faith in ourselves and in the journey, we are on. It's about believing that tough times will pass and that we have the inner resources to persevere. By staying positive, practicing self-care, and remaining hopeful, we can navigate through any storm that comes our way. Remember, resilience is not about avoiding hardships but about facing them with grace, courage, and determination.

Gratitude for the Journey

As I sit here reflecting on the journey that has brought me to this moment, I can't help but feel overwhelming gratitude. The path to self-discovery and personal growth has been filled with twists and turns, challenges, and triumphs. I am grateful for every experience, both positive and negative, as they have shaped me into the person I am today.

Looking back on the milestones and turning points that marked my journey, I realize that each obstacle I faced only served to strengthen my resolve and deepen my understanding of myself. The moments of doubt and uncertainty pushed me to dig deep and find the courage to keep moving forward, even when the road ahead seemed dark and overwhelming.

Throughout this journey, I have learned the power of resilience, the importance of self-compassion, and the beauty of embracing vulnerability. I have discovered that true strength lies in being open to the lesson's life has to offer, even when they come in unexpected and sometimes painful ways.

As I close this chapter of my life and look towards the future, I am filled with a sense of peace and gratitude. Gratitude for the people who have supported me along the way, for the challenges that have taught me valuable lessons, and for the growth that has come from embracing each moment, even the difficult ones.

This journey has not always been easy, but it has been fulfilling in ways I never could have imagined. I am grateful for every step, every stumble, and every moment of triumph. As I embark on the next chapter of my life, I do so with a heart full of gratitude for the journey that has brought me to this point.

Gratitude and Moving Forward: Expressing thanks for the journey so far while looking ahead to what lies ahead

As I reflect on the journey I've been on, I can't help but feel a sense of gratitude for all the experiences that have shaped me into the person I am today. From the challenges that evaluated my resilience to the moments of joy that filled my heart, each step along the way has been a part of my growth and evolution.

I am thankful for the lessons I've learned, even when they were hard-fought and difficult to swallow. They have taught me perseverance, patience, and the importance of staying true to myself in the face of adversity. Each setback has been a steppingstone to greater understanding and resilience, showing me that strength is not defined by the absence of struggle but by the ability to rise above it.

Looking ahead, I am filled with a sense of hope and anticipation for what the future holds. While the path may be uncertain and the challenges ahead may be overwhelming, I carry with me the wisdom and insights gained from my past experiences. I know that whatever obstacles come my way, I have the inner strength and resilience to face them and emerge stronger on the other side.

So, as I express gratitude for the journey so far, I also look forward with excitement and determination to the road ahead. With a grateful heart and a resilient spirit, I am ready to embrace whatever the future may bring, knowing that each new experience is an opportunity for growth and self-discovery.

My book is full of gratitude. I want to express my deepest thanks to the Holy Spirit, my parents, my family, and everyone who has impacted my life, both negatively and positively. To my three children,

DeJaun, Sierra, and my Guardian Angel, Tierra: you have made this journey meaningful to me. To my two grandchildren, Lil DeJaun and DeYaun: I cherish all the moments we share. To MC, the special person who has become an integral part of my journey. Your unwavering support, love, and companionship have inspired me to embrace new adventures and write the next chapter of our story together. Here's to the incredible journey ahead and the countless memories we will create side by side. Thank you for being my partner and my inspiration.

www.ingramcontent.com/pod-product-compliance
Lightning Source LLC
Chambersburg PA
CBHW071002120626
46546CB00003B/890

* 9 7 8 1 9 6 1 6 7 3 0 7 6 *